Grail

GRAIL

John Constable

incantations, spells, meditations

First published in 2022
Blue Cedar Printworks, Silver Street, Glastonbury BA6 8BS

A catalogue record for this book is available from the British library.

ISBN: 978-1-913325-13-8

IESUS
MARIA

carved on the wall of Our Lady's Chapel, Glastonbury Abbey

In 63 AD twelve disciples came to Britain to teach the Incarnation of Jesus Christ. They were led by Joseph of Arimathea who had buried The Lord. The King refused to convert to the new faith but, seeing that they had come so far and impressed by their exemplary behaviour, granted them an island surrounded by woods and marshes called Ynys Witrin... Successive Kings gave each of the saints a portion of land. These became known as The Twelve Hides. Having lived in the wilderness, they had a vision of the Angel Gabriel who showed them the place for a church dedicated to the Blessed Virgin… They built a simple church of wattle which was graced by God with many miracles…

De antiquitate Glastoniensis ecclesiae, William of Malmesbury c. 1130 (from an amended copy c.1250)

I have been dead. I have been alive. I am Taliesin.

The Mabinogi

also by John Constable

SHA-MANIC PLAYS
THE SOUTHWARK MYSTERIES
SPARK IN THE DARK

*

GORMENGHAST
(stage adaptation of the Mervyn Peake Trilogy)

*

SECRET BANKSIDE
(Walks In The Outlaw Borough)

Contents

The Way In

Here is a magical artefact, a book of incantations, spells and meditations to open the pathways. It charts my initiation into The Grail and the Mysteries of Avalon during a year of life in Glastonbury.

Here Arthur and Merlin step out of the Celtic Dreamtime, charging the landscape with mythic resonance. Joseph of Arimathea sails from The Holy Land, bearing the spear that pierced Christ on the cross and The Chalice that received His blood. On Wearyall Hill his staff takes root and flowers, becomes the Glastonbury Thorn. The Chalice he buries on Chalice Hill; the waters of a spring are stained red with blood. A pagan chieftain grants him 'Twelve Hides' of land. He builds a wattle-and-daub church...[1]

And did those feet in ancient times
walk upon England's mountains green? [2]

Time opens into Eternity, and Jesus is here in person with his uncle, Joseph the tin-trader. The Boy God initiated into the Druid Mysteries. Some say that wattle church was built not by Joseph but by the hand of God, that Jesus dedicated it to his Mother, and that The Mother of God Herself is buried here in the ruined Abbey. Or that during his 'missing years' Jesus returned with Mary Magdalene and their love-child.

And looming over all, The Tor, with its Blood and White Springs and neolithic Dragon Lines. Here the Old Gods rule. Gwyn ap Nudd holds court in the Underworld, Annwn, the fairy castle that guards the Cauldron of Inspiration.

Here ancient heathen myths merge with Christian mysticism to conceive The Holy Grail, the elusive cup that heals all ills, the source of physical sustenance and spiritual transformation.

We each have a personal Quest for The Grail, our own vision of what it is and how to receive it. Mine came into vivid focus during my first year of living in Glastonbury, having made many pilgrimages to this 'holiest earth' – and having just completed a 23 year magical work in south London. This book maps my initiation, a new way into the old Mysteries, a working with my Spirit Guide to make new connections, to open the neural pathways.

It's intended to evoke an authentic initiation in You, Dear Reader. You're welcome to use the spells and incantations in your own magical work. They are activated by being spoken aloud with intent. You're advised to first read them in silence, so you know what you're getting into! They are ruled by One Iron Law: that we wish for others only what we would wish for ourselves. Because what we do unto others, ultimately we do to ourselves. Be firm. Be kind.

These meditations and vignettes, they too are an integral part of a single spell. A re-enchantment. An act of reconciliation, healing and restoration.

A re-membering.

Today, in the ruins of Glastonbury Abbey, a sign marks where the monks found the bones of King Arthur and Queen Guinevere in 1191 AD. They were reburied below the High Altar in 1278 in the presence of King

Edward I and Queen Eleanor. The discovery of 'Arthur's grave' helped raise funds to rebuild The Abbey after the Old Church burnt down in 1184. It may also have suited the Plantagenet Kings to dispel the myth of a semi-divine Celtic chieftain who would return to save the land, as implied in the medieval Welsh *Black Book of Carmarthen*: 'Not wise (the thought) a grave for Arthur.' [3] In the *Vita Merlini*, the wounded King is borne away in a boat to be healed by Morgan on the Isle of Avalon.[4]

Many Glastonbury legends were recorded and embellished by monastic scribes during the 12th and early 13th centuries when The Abbey was eager to shore up its prestige – and a spiritual lineage to rival Rome.

Joseph of Arimathea is said to have built his wattle church on the site of Our Lady's Chapel, at the west end of the now ruined Abbey, thereby establishing the first Christian community in the British Isles. According to the visionary antiquarian John Michell, the Lady Chapel and Great Church precisely embody the proportions of The New Jerusalem, The City of God in *The Book of Revelation*. The chapel was constructed in the form of a *vesica piscis*, interlocking circles with the centre of one on the circumference of the other, forming the mystical Christian symbol of the fish.

In the Welsh Triads, Glastonbury Abbey is named as one of three monastic communities charged with having a 'perpetual choir', with relays of monks keeping up a continuous chant. Michell identifies these choirs with the chosen ones who 'sang a new song' in *The Book of Revelation*, and suggests that 'when the song changed, a new age began.' [5] He reminds us that 'chanting' is the root of 'enchantment' and that:

The Grail Legend is of a former enchantment, now broken, which will one day be restored. One day the lost Grail will be found…[6]

The Christian and pagan elements of Avalon are often seen as being in opposition or outright conflict. The 7th century monk St Collen is said to have banished Gwyn-ap-Nudd from The Tor, using holy water to exorcise his chimerical fairy kingdom. The fairies and their heathen followers claimed their revenge with the earthquake which destroyed the old St Michael's church in 1275 AD. The church on the summit of The Tor was rebuilt but desecrated following the Reformation. Today, only the tower remains standing. In 1539, during the violent destruction of Glastonbury Abbey, the last Abbot, Richard Whiting, was hanged, drawn and quartered with two of his brother monks on The Tor in a blasphemous parody of the crucifixion.

The early 20th century occultist Dion Fortune divided the New Avalonians into 'Abbey People' and 'Tor People'. In *A Glastonbury Romance*, her contemporary John Cowper Powys envisages The Abbey and The Tor as embodying the conflict between Christianity and the old heathen gods. I see them rather as Blakean contraries, each with their unique place in an Eternity vast, capacious and empty enough to hold every being, every thought, every deed.

Without Contraries is no progression… Opposition is True Friendship.[7]

I live and work at the nexus of Poetry, Theatre and Magic.

On the 23rd November 1996 I embarked on a 23-year magical work at Cross Bones Graveyard in south London. In my shamanic John Crow persona I channelled the spirit of The Goose, a medieval sex worker licensed by a Bishop to work in church-owned brothels yet buried in the unconsecrated Cross Bones Yard. Speaking in verse, The Goose revealed Herself as a channel of The Magdalene, Isis, Kwan Yin and the 'Outcast Goddess'. I soon discovered that, when I performed these verses aloud, I reconnected with the current and entered the same heightened states in which they were received. They conveyed me beyond their literal meanings into the inexpressible beauty and grace of The Goose Spirit, Her 'shining emptiness'.

The Goose and Crow texts grew into *The Southwark Mysteries* – a cycle of poems, then a Mystery Play performed in Shakespeare's Globe and Southwark Cathedral. They in turn gave rise to the annual *Halloween of Cross Bones* rituals and the Vigils held at the graveyard gates on the 23rd of every month. These literary and magical works underpinned an activist campaign which saw Cross Bones transformed from a derelict industrial site into a shrine and a garden of remembrance for sex workers and outcasts.

On 23rd November 2019, the 23rd anniversary of the original 'Goose Night', I conducted my last Vigil, completing the work. In July 2020, with Katy Kaos, my wife and co-practitioner, I vowed to walk The Goose around these islands, to let Her lead us where She would. She'd already shown how every place is holy if you know where – and how – to look. She led us here.

Glastonbury called. We answered, trusting the Universe to open a new, maybe the last, chapter in our lives. Six weeks later we were living here, in the place we're meant to be. Having trusted The Goose to find us a place, we weren't too surprised to discover we were in the old red-light district, on the corner of the former Grope Cunt Lane!

I proceeded to immerse myself in this mythic landscape. The natural way to get to know the spirits of place is to draw them into conversation, a creative exchange. As winter closed in, I walked The Goose around the deserted streets of a town in lock-down. The space and silence helped us to tune into Glastonbury's subtle astral and etheric forms.

On the Full Moon of 30th December 2020, a Blue Moon, I asked The Goose for a spell to open the pathways.

She gave me three.

[1] The earliest sources for the founding of the Old Church give the date as 37 or 63 AD. St Augustine's letter to Pope Gregory (c. 600, quoted in a biography of St Dunstan c. 1000) states that it was '… a church constructed by no human art, but by the hands of Christ Himself… as sacred to Himself, and to Mary, the Mother of God.'

[2] *Jerusalem* (from the poem *Milton*), William Blake

[3] *The Black Book of Carmarthen*, translated by John Rhys

[4] *Vita Merlini*, Geoffrey of Monmouth

[5] *City of Revelation*, John Michell

[6] *New Light On The Ancient Mystery of Glastonbury*, John Michell

[7] *The Marriage of Heaven and Hell*, William Blake

A Little Spell of Unforgetting

for Paul Weston

A clamour! Bleeding lances
And the beat of the tambour.
Out of the ruin The Earth calls Time: No More!

No more let false enchantment
Beguile this ravished land.
The Time of the Remembering is at hand.

By the elemental Cauldron
Hollowed deep within The Tor,
Gwyn ap Nudd is opening the Door.

Merlin casts upon the waters,
Dragons writhing in the deep.
As on The Isle of Avalon we sleep.

In a boat of fog and faery,
Gliding on the Glassy Lake,
Arthur dreams the dream wherein we wake.

By the full moon, Joseph
Plants The Chalice in the mud.
And Lo! The spring that flows there, wells with blood.

Our Lady in Her Chapel
Unfolds God's Female Part
In a pulse of Love to open up the Heart.

Here the Christ Child quickens
In Each Life to reveal
The Work, and the Play, and the Way for our
broken World to heal.

Now every stricken healer
In the shadow of The Tor
Let The Grail replenish and restore.

In the gone, forever bell-tower
The bells their changes ring.
The many voices of The One, Perpetual Choir, sing.

The One made Many to consort,
Their Songs of Liberty
Light up the Unconditioned Mind: in Time, Eternity.

The Wound

The Chalice passes into the keeping of Joseph's descendents, the lineage of The Fisher Kings. According to local legends it's in an invisible castle on Wearyall Hill, or concealed in an underground chamber under Chalice Hill. Some have had visions of a golden cup rising effulgent over the Tor.

King Fisherman, also known as The Fisher King, languishes from a festering wound. The spear that delivered 'the dolorous stroke' is often identified with the Spear of Longinus which pierced Jesus as he hung on the cross. This was another holy relic supposedly brought here by Joseph of Arimathea. The appearance and 'service' of The Grail is preceded by a procession of enigmatic totems, including a spear whose pointed tip still bleeds.

The Fisher King is wounded in the groin. The explicitly sexual nature of the injury links it with ancient fertility rites: the land itself becomes a barren waste, awaiting an act of healing and restoration. The wound, and the devastation it causes, can only be healed by asking the enigmatic question: 'Whom does it serve?'

In *From Ritual to Romance* Jessie L. Weston connects The Fisher King with the Divine Kings of pagan rituals. In his notes on *The Waste Land*, T. S. Eliot acknowledges his debt to 'Miss Weston's Book' for the title, plan and symbolism of his 1922 poem.

A century later, the Waste Land still cries out for healing. And in an Age when masculinity is often perceived as toxic, the healing of wounded manhood –

sexually, psychologically and spiritually – is an essential part of the Work (and the Play).

And, no less, the restoration of the feminine with Her own agency and sovereignty.

The second of the magical texts received on the night of the December Blue Moon is a song-spell for the healing of The Fisher King. Like all these spells and incantations it seemed to write itself, without the intervention of my conscious mind. Only when I shaped and polished the verses and did more research, did I recognise their arcane references and resonances.

The Knights of The Grail Quest had to endure an all-night vigil in the Chapel Perilous, during which their faith was tested with visions of demonic orgies.

'The Queen' could refer to Guinevere or to The Queen of Heaven exiled by patriarchal religion.

'The soul of sweet delight can never be defiled' is a direct quote from Blake's *Proverbs of Hell.*

In *Avalon of The Heart* Dion Fortune identifies The Cup (The Grail) and The Sword (Excalibur) as archetypes of female and male energies.

In *Camelot and the Vision of Albion* Geoffrey Ashe recalls the Greek myths of 'The Isles of the Blessed', the islands in the West where Cronos, having been overthrown and exiled by Zeus, sleeps peacefully, never growing old. These 'Fortunate Isles' were later associated with the Isle of Avalon, where Arthur is brought to be healed. The island, formed by four hills – Glastonbury Tor, Chalice Hill, Wearyall Hill and St Edmund's Hill – would have been visible from far away, rising above the lakes and marshes.

Sing, Sing The Fisher King

Sing, sing The Fisher King,
Sing for the healing of the wound in him.
Sing, sing The Fisher King,
Sing for the healing of the wound within.

Sing for The Waste Land, ragged and torn,
In the long night watch before the bright dawn.

Sing, sing The Fisher King,
Sing for the healing of the wound in him.
Sing, sing The Fisher King,
Sing for the healing of the wound within.

Sing for The Queen cast out in the wild,
For the soul of sweet delight can never be defiled.

Sing, sing The Fisher King,
Sing for the healing of the wound in him.
Sing, sing The Fisher King,
Sing for the healing of the wound within.

Sing for the serving of the Holy Grail,
And for The Holy Fool who lives to tell the tale.

Sing, sing The Fisher King,
Sing for the healing of the wound in him.
Sing, sing The Fisher King,
Sing for the healing of the wound within.

Sing for the balance in the Cup and the Sword,
And for the asking that he be restored.

Sing, sing The Fisher King,
Sing for the healing of the wound in him.
Sing, sing The Fisher King,
Sing for the healing of the wound within.

Sing for the healing in The Isles of the Blessed.
Sing for The Healing, and let go the rest.

Orientation

From our tiny garden, we see the tower of St John the Baptist rising above the rooftops. The window at the top of the stairs gives a view of The Tor, except in summer when it's hidden by leafy trees in The Abbey. Our bedroom looks onto St Benedict's church. Our initial co-ordinates.

In 1972, a year after my first visit here, I'd bought a pamphlet: *Glastonbury: A Study In Patterns*. There was an essay on the sacred geometry of The Abbey by John Michell, a seminal influence who later became a friend. In September 2020, unpacking our boxes after the move, I found the pamphlet, opened it at John's article, and read:

From St Benedict's a line extended through The Abbey, along Dod Lane and past the foot of the Tor… and strikes the centre of Stonehenge… the name Dod in Dod Lane refers both to the word for death and to the Egyptian Thoth or Mercury. Dod Lane is part of a mercurial spirit path, the bed of an invisible stream along which the souls of the dead are conveyed on their passage to Avalon, the western Isle.[1]

Our new home is just south of this Dod Line.

According to hermetic tradition, the Egyptian god Thoth is the original author of The Tarot. One tale tells how he devised the Major Arcana to chart a path of initiation into The Mysteries. He was teaching his students when the pack fell to the ground: the cards scattered. Thoth seized on this random happening to open a new pathway of divination.

The third Blue Moon Spell is an invocation to Thoth (Dod), framed in the imagery of The Tarot. It was not the result of a literal Tarot reading; rather that certain cards presented themselves in my mind to offer a mythic 'reading' of Avalon.

For the opening two stanzas, the Tarot Cards follow their procession in the Major Arcana: The Fool, The Magician, The High Priestess.

The cards in the third stanza disrupt the natural order: The Hanged Man, The Tower, The Devil.

The closing stanzas call on Dod to perform an act of rebalancing and restoration by selecting certain cards: Fortitude (or 'Strength', 'Lust' in the Crowley pack), The Star, The Moon and The Sun.

[1] *Glastonbury Abbey: A solar instrument of former science*, John Michell. Published in *Glastonbury A Study In Patterns* (RILKO 1969)

Dod Cut The Cards

Dod cut the cards for the Avalon Reading:
    The Holy Fool walking on air.
Above him: The Mage who lives up the Lane
    Calling from Dod knows where.

Below him: The Priestess opens the way
    To the nurturing darkness within
And the light that shines on when we are gone
    As it shines before we begin.

Then the deck get stacked; the message get scrambled:
    The Hanged Man strung up on the Tor,
And all fall down, save only The Tower
    And plague, The Devil and war.

Dod, shuffle the pack. Give Strength in the woman
    To temper the lion's lust.
The Star to mingle the blood and white streams
    And The Moon to dream us

As the playful children
    We once were and shall become,
Shining, laughing, dancing
    In the gardens of The Sun.

On Protection

At its best, Glastonbury is a tolerant, open-minded community where diverse spiritual beliefs and practices co-exist in harmony. But, as we say in these parts, 'the brighter the sun the stronger the shadow'. When I moved here, old-timers warned me that our town had been through a dark and divisive year. There were grim tales of power struggles, bullying and mind-control.

Then the pandemic took hold and the town went into lockdown. No-one knew what was happening, which didn't stop them from having opinions. Even as the death-toll rose and a public health emergency loomed, some old hippies hopped into bed with neo-Nazis, retreating into a parallel universe in which billionaire Bill Gates had created a 'virus hoax' so as to inject us all with microchips. These would then be activated by 5G mobile microwaves turning us all into Gates' puppets and zombies. (Having spent a third of my life channelling the spirit of a medieval sex worker, it was odd to find myself cast as the Voice of Reason, extolling the virtues of peer-reviewed science!)

Factor in the new Christs and Crowleys, and the vulnerable seekers whose minds get blown by all this high-voltage psychic energy, and it's no surprise to find the lowest levels of the Avalonian Astral Plane crawling with disturbed, predatory thought-forms.

It can seem as if every other Glastonbury resident is engaged in some sort of magical practice. No doubt some are using magic in an attempt to exert power over others or to do them ill. How can we best protect ourselves from their spells, or simply from their negative thoughts and energies? We can begin by putting our own houses in order.

I once spent an entrancing Sunday afternoon talking Magic and Art with Alan Moore at his home in Northampton. We strove to outdo each other in denouncing those who use Magic to manipulate others. He told me how some creep had once asked him for a love-charm or potion to make a woman desire him. Alan had sarcastically suggested Rohypnol, the notorious date-rape drug. His point being that to cast a spell on another is itself an act of rape: rape of the psyche, the spirit.

Most children are to some degree fluent in the art of 'magical thinking', the belief that our thoughts and actions can cause sympathetic responses and effects in the external world. It may be as simple as counting paving-stones, not stepping on the cracks, or relying on superstitious sayings to counter bad omens. 'Good morning, Mr Magpie, how's your wife today?'

This child-like way of perceiving and interacting with the world often persists into adult life with varying results. It's the basis of diverse magical and religious practices, of prayers, spells and ritual observances. However it's also associated with many psychological disorders, the idea that our thoughts or actions can cause certain things to happen, or prevent them from happening, even when there is no causal relationship.

Magical thinking and superstition can be seen as ways of dealing with our fear of the unknown, of exerting some sort of order and influence on things over which we have little control or understanding.

Indeed, it may not be too fanciful to consider that most magical practices are ultimately grounded in childhood fears and insecurities.

Between the age of seven and nine I endured nightly poltergeist activity. It'd begin with subtle, familiar noises – creaky floorboards or a tapping at the window – but would soon progress to more pronounced yet inexplicable sounds. I still recall a loud detonation from inside a wardrobe, powerful enough for the doors to burst open. On another occasion I was startled by a voice addressing me directly. Such paranormal activities seemed to occur when I was in the liminal state between sleep and waking. On several occasions I had to pinch myself to check that I was fully awake; I always was – and still the noises and voices persisted. I've spoken to other magical practitioners who were able to recall incidents in childhood which challenged their acceptance of consensual reality, impelling them to deal with this alternate magical world in which everything is connected.

In my own case, it was the sense that there was something lurking 'out there' beyond our normal powers of comprehension, and that sooner or later I would have to confront it or else live in its shadow. In my late teens when I lived in a cottage in Wales I had to walk home (or run, when I lost my nerve) for several miles up a country line, aware of every snapping twig, every bestial grunt. One night the sheep formed a circle to bleat at the full moon. The howl of a dog – or was it a wolf? A werewolf? A dire wolf? Alone in the Welsh hills, with no-one for miles around, it's easy to let your imagination run wild.

I think that it was this need to confront and conquer these debilitating terrors that impelled me to experiment first with LSD and other psychedelics, then with magic. It was as if I needed to take that leap into an Unknown in which I had no choice but to face whatever was 'out there' (or, worse, 'in here', in the contents of my own psyche). Then when I was older The Goose came and I became her John Crow shaman and had no choice but to walk the walk as best I could.

Shamanism is not an alternative life-style choice or proof that we're somehow superior beings. On the contrary, shamanistic initiations often arise from our imperfections and inadequacies. We need something powerful enough to shake down our fears of madness and death. If we get it right we find the firmness, love and vision to go beyond.

So it's not surprising that so much magical practice is concerned with protecting ourselves from other entities, incarnate or discarnate. We trust in amulets, spoken formulae, magic circles, pentagrams and other symbols to defend us from curses and hexes. In extreme cases, for our own peace of mind, it may help to perform a ritual to banish negative influences, employ a 'magic mirror' technique to reflect the hex back to its origin, or create a poppet to receive the curse in our place. It you do, do it with the absolute certainty that it *will* be done, *is* done.

Yet herein lies the curious paradox at the heart of all magical battles. The success of a curse or hex depends on the credulity of the victim. That's why those in the business of cursing and hexing others will often deploy occult signs or symbols to let their intended victims know. In fact, anyone who mouths off about how they've put a spell on you is very unlikely to have the power or the skill to do you serious harm. Their best hope is to plant seeds of fear and doubt in your mind; as with any other psychic contents, if you feed and water them, they'll grow. The danger is that, in striving to resist or banish a curse, you accidentally empower it with your own psychic energy.

The other problem with talismans and the like is that you can come to depend too much on them. What happens if you lose your amulet? Or, worse, if your deadly enemy gets hold of it?

A month or so after my first encounter with my spirit guide, I visited Bali where I bought myself a shaman's scarf. It was an *ikat* weave, pale blue with white markings, and woven into it were spirit forms, tiny homunculi. Over the next few years, I wore that scarf for all the public ceremonies I conducted – for *The Halloween of Cross Bones* and other rituals performed at the graveyard, at Stonehenge, at Glastonbury, and at many a pagan site and festival.

Then I lost it at *Earth Spirit.* The entire site was like a mud-pit and the scarf, being abnormally long, kept slipping off my neck and dragging in the mud. All through the night I was constantly retrieving and adjusting it. At dawn, it was gone, as if it had slid off and snaked away into the earth. It took time to get over the feeling that, without it, I was unprotected and would have to renounce the magical path. Gradually it struck me that, by investing so much power in a physical object and relying on it to protect me, I was actually making myself more vulnerable.

When The Goose first took hold of John Crow she came freighted with secret histories, fraught with traumatic memories of degradation and abuse. She was a channel for many brutalised, disturbed spirits. That night could easily have turned into a bad trip, a descent into psychosis.

I'd approached it as a vision quest and an act of experimental writing. I was aware that I was dabbling in mediumship, though I hadn't expected the automatic writing to emerge in such vivid, poetic forms. Nor had I expected a visitation from a spirit with such an intricate inner life, or lives. But I had anticipated that I could be opening myself up to all manner of Astral entities, and had taken a few simple precautions. I did a ritual purification, bathing and anointing with oils. I lit candles and incense before my altar to Kwan Yin, prostrating before Her, repeating 'I am nothing. Thou Art, Kwan Yin. Free from fear.' – and chanting the *Heart Sutra* again and again.

The *Heart Sutra* transmits the enlightened insight of the Bodhisattva who, having attained Enlightenment, vows to forego their own Nirvana for so long as a single ant is bound by suffering. The Bodhisattva looks down into the building blocks of perception, seeing their intrinsic emptiness and evanescence.

In Tibetan Buddhist teachings, Avalokiteśvara weeps to see the suffering of all beings; one of the tears becomes Tara. The teachings of the compassionate Bodhisattva crossed the Himalayas to China, cross-pollinating with Taoism and a local fertility goddess beloved by fishermen. Katy and I visited a cave in Thailand where Her effigy is surrounded by red phallic offerings. In this form She is Kwan Yin (Japanese: Kannon), the Goddess of Compassion.

During a year living in Japan (1977-78) I'd learned to chant the *Heart Sutra* in Japanese:

Ma Ka Han Nya Ha Ra Mi Ta Shin Gyo…

It's a shimmering invocation and evocation of 'No-thing-ness' – not at all the same thing as 'nothing', which is itself a 'thing', a name, a mind-form. The *Heart Sutra* calmly exposes the impermanence and insubstantiality of all names and forms:

There is no eye, no ear, no nose, no tongue, no touch, no sight, no sound, no smell, no taste, no object of touch…

culminating in the negation of even the key precepts of Buddhism:

No pain, no end of pain, no Noble Path to lead from Pain, no realisation to attain. Attainment too is empty.

The conceptual paradoxes of the text are fascinating in themselves, disrupting the mind's ceaseless attempts to grab hold of itself, much like a Zen *koan*.

The power of the chant is embodied in the sounds themselves, in the trance-like rhythms and vibrations modulated by the repetitive syllable *Mu* ('No' - denying the reality of everything we can name).

None of which is to deny the beauty of this transient world, or to gloss over its terrors, but simply to realise that these beauties and terrors, these microcosms, are fleeting manifestations of a macrocosm that itself arises and vanishes without trace.

In shining emptiness.

So best not to get too hung up on protecting ourselves psychically, lest we empower the very thing from which we think we need protecting. The trick is to cultivate the shining emptiness in which there is no fear of possession or psychic attack by alien entities, because there's nothing for anything to attach to.

When we first work with the discipline of shining emptiness, we use it to observe external phenomena without getting attached or entangled in them. This can then be used to protect us from what we may perceive as hostile entities. As the practice evolves, we find we can apply this technique to our own thoughts, emotions and physical sensations, seeing how we can get bound up in them, weaving them together to construct a 'self'.

In its place, there's nothing wrong with an ego. It helps us navigate the barrage of sense impressions to which we're exposed every nano-second, and to construct our own maps and models of reality. To fixate on transcending, or worse still destroying, our ego is itself an act of monstrous egotism and self-obsession.

The problem with the ego only arises when we start believing it's *all* we are, that we're somehow hermetically sealed off from the rest of existence and consciousness. By dispassionately observing our own sensations, and the emotional responses and thought-forms they elicit, we can gently dissolve the boundaries that divide us from Big Mind / No-Mind.

This technique enabled me to simultaneously channel The Goose and John Crow, the female and male spirits, to record their interactions and to perform their magical works over many years without suffering serious psychological damage.

For a magical cycle of thirteen years I conducted *The Halloween of Cross Bones* rituals in which we worked with the spirits of the outcast dead. Participants were given a ribbon bearing the name of someone buried in Cross Bones Yard. They were invited to adopt their spirit for the evening, and to release it when they tied the ribbon to the shrine at the gates. One year, a participant asked John Crow: 'Will we get possessed.'

'Only by ourselves', quoth Crow.

On one level, this entire book can be read as a crafty banishing ritual, a trick to set us free from ourselves. Once we've done that, there's not a Black Magician in town can touch us!

Christ Mass

Christmas Day in the locked-down
Ghost Town: four riderless horses
hitched by The George and Pilgrim.

A New Age Heretic
chalks on the pavement
BILL GATES IS INNOCENT.

By a burning church, the monks unearth
bones of doubtful provenance
again, in vain.

Arthur serves hot cacao
to flagging Questers. Guinevere
bejewels their Third Eyes.

A truck pulls up and down
steps Venus, on her way to becoming
Shee.

Jesus and his mates
bopping to the beatbox
by the Market

Cross.

The Spoils of Annwn

In his poem *The Spoils of Annwn* the archetypal Welsh Bard Taliesin relates how he accompanied Arthur and his war band on a raid to seize the Cauldron of *Awen* or Poetic Inspiration from Annwn (*Annwfyn*), the Celtic Underworld.

> *My poetry from the cauldron it was uttered.*
> *From the breath of nine maidens it was kindled.*
> *The cauldron of the Chief of Annwfyn: what is its fashion?*
> *A dark ridge around its border and pearls.*
> *It does not boil the food of a coward; it has not been destined.*[1]

The Cauldron is guarded in the fairy fortress of Caer Sidi, 'the prison of Gweir'. A perilous quest, evidently. Only seven of the raiding party return alive.

Taliesin was a Welsh Bard of the 6th century, working within an oral tradition stretching back millennia. His poems were only written down in the 14th century, by Christian scribes who freely applied their own gloss. Many of the works attributed to him may be the work of his contemporaries – the name Taliesin having become an honorific title bestowed on particularly gifted Bards. In the medieval texts Taliesin is often referred to as *Taliesin Ben Beirdd* (colloquial translation: 'Taliesin, Top Bard').

A Song Concerning the Sons of Llyr ab Brochwel Powys (poem XIV in *The Book of Taliesin*) evokes Caer Sidi as a land of Eternal Youth, where Taliesin claims and takes his Bardic 'Seat' or 'Chair'.

The following evocation is my response to the those two Taliesin originals. Since I began writing mystical verses around the time of my teenage psychedelic initiation in North Wales I've honoured Taliesin as the archetypal Bard, the patron of all who follow in the quest for Poetic Vision and psychic transformation.

We who would drink of The Cauldron are risking not only our bodies but our minds. Being at one with the creative principle may easily overwhelm with madness and delusion. My incantation expresses the importance of being at once connected and unattached, of fully entering into the vision without fixating on any aspect of it. The aim is not only to survive our journey to the Other World, but to return with the 'spoils'.

And the prize is great. When we are truly in our Seat, our Chair, our place, we are deeply, intimately connected with all of existence.

[1] *Preiddeu Annwn*, The Spoils of Annwn, trans. Sarah Higley Robbins Library Digital Projects / The Camelot Project, 2007

Perfect is my Chair in Caer Sidi

after Taliesin

In the Revolving Castle, whose doors open
not in the fixed, mapped, X-marked spots,

but in the cracks, the quirks and quarks
that shift their shapes to quake the Castle Walls.

If I had to tell it to the Scientist,
I'd say the Castle Doors are chemical

receptors – you key in...
With a twist: when you're in, you're It.

Be still in the spin of the Whirligig Castle,
cross-eyed to see the lip in the skin

and key in… Next twist:
if you fix on anything, you get fixed.

Be nothing at the hub of the Turning Castle. See
what you shall see, and return in Poetry.

In the living heart of the Spiral Castle
I drink

from the cauldron, warmed
by the breath of nine Muses.

And what I drink, I Am.
I Am

Sky, am Raven
who fly me; a chuckle of sparrows;

the waxing moon, and the sun
who seed them.

And, knowing that Castle Door is always open –
not on some fabled island in the West

but close as breath and heartbeat,
as hand on moss and stone –

in the Fairy Castle, I Am.

Perfect is my Chair in Caer Sidi.

On Pilgrimage

The most celebrated pilgrimage in English history and literature is recorded, envisioned, by Geoffrey Chaucer. *The Canterbury Tales* charts the journey of a group of pilgrims drawn from all strata of late 14th century English society – the noble Knight, the lusty Wife of Bath, the Pardoner, the Monk and other representatives of the clergy, down to the bawdy drunken Miller with his scurrilous tale. They're on their way to Canterbury, to the tomb and shrine of Thomas Becket, murdered in his own Cathedral on the orders of King Henry II. In July 1174 the King himself made the pilgrimage to Canterbury to perform a penance for the murder of the Archbishop. He made a public confession, was beaten by monks and kept vigil at Becket's tomb. By Chaucer's time the cult of Becket and the miraculous cures associated with his shrine drew crowds of ordinary people.

Aside from its deep religious significance, the pilgrimage also created a subversive subculture in which people could share ideas that challenged the established order. Thus, at the suggestion of Landlord Harry Bailly who hosts their supper at The Tabard Inn in Southwark, Chaucer's pilgrims tell each other stories – of forbidden love and illicit sex, of greedy men tricked by Death – creating a profane compliment to their sacred journey. Here is an alternative, earthy folk-religion, transmitted not from pulpits but in tales told and songs sung at the Traveller's Inn.

The Pilgrimage to Glastonbury goes back even further than Chaucer or Becket. In the 6th and 7th centuries it drew Irish saints like St Patrick and St Bride. Pilgrims were attracted to The Abbey as a fount of spiritual knowledge, blessed with sacred relics and 'the holiest erthe in England', a centre of Celtic Christianity with a time-honoured tradition to rival even Rome. The discovery of Arthur and Guinevere's bones in the Abbey cemetery in 1191 provided an added attraction.

Medieval pilgrims entered by the great North Gate, within which were displayed pages from *Magna Tabula Glastonensis.*[1] Many would have made a long and difficult journey, some barefoot and wearing hair-shirts or with flagellants' whips of penance. They came seeking physical healing and spiritual sustenance, knowledge and insight – and a reduction of the sentence to be served in purgatory before their promised ascent to Heaven. The Abbey's holy relics and St Joseph's Spring, which still trickles in the well by his chapel, were believed to have curative powers.

Hospitals and hostelries opened in the town, offering shelter to the weary pilgrim. One such Pilgrims Hospital was founded in 1250. In the 15th century it was rebuilt as the Magdalene Almshouses for the parish poor, which can still be seen just off Magdalene Street. The Pilgrims Inn, later The George and Pilgrims Inn, opened in the late 15th century by the Market Cross.

On Silver Street, pilgrims could buy badges, medallions, crucifixes and silver devotional tokens to keep as mementos or to offer at one of the shrines in The Abbey. They could also purchase amphorae to gather water from the holy well and wax effigies of various body-parts in need of healing. Given the prevalence of the pox, it's likely that little wax images of sexual parts were in high demand. One imagines the medieval street, with shops selling rosaries, icons and other devotional emblems, perhaps including representations of The Grail or the Bleeding Lance! As we cross-fade back to the present, we find similar shops in the High Street selling faerie statuettes or yantra lampshades to a new generation of pilgrims.

Everything changes. Nothing changes.

Even when we're simply on holiday, we behave differently. Everything is heightened, alive with emotional connections. We notice tiny, exquisite details that, back home, we'd pass without a second glance, and strike up random conversations with complete strangers, which are sometimes the beginning of enduring friendships.

All this is amplified and magnified on pilgrimage, where we are consciously moving towards a destination we've invested with spiritual significance. Everything that happens, everyone we meet, every new landscape, every bird or beast, every thought and dream becomes a numinous portent, an intricate part of the whole unfolding. And because we're paying attention, we discover new patterns, new connections. Even if we're not graced with a vision of The Grail or Our Lady, the very act of mindful journeying can enable us to see the world anew.

On such spiritual journeys we're often reminded of our own transience. With every day the landscape changes, revealing new stages of the journey, mountains to climb, rivers to ford, challenges to overcome. Our inner life similarly undergoes reversals, upheavals, obstacles, dark nights of the soul. As we press on, despite our doubts, our irritations, our aching legs, we develop the fortitude and resilience to endure the tests and trials that life presents. And it gradually dawns on us that the beauty of creation is inextricably bound up with its fleeting nature.

And those pilgrims like us, who come and stay, we need to constantly remind ourself of the great truth that is easily lost in glib repetition:

We're just passing through.

Katy and I had visited Glastonbury many times on pilgrimage or simply on the way to see my family in the West Country. We always enjoyed reconnecting with the magic of the town and the land, though we used to joke: 'Couldn't live here!' Our mercurial temperaments needed grounding in the grit of London life. Glastonbury seemed too… well, bonkers!

In July 2020, between lock-downs, we came here for my birthday, staying with our friends Sally and James North on Silver Street. On an impulse I posted on the Glastonbury Notice Board: 'Creative couple looking to rent...' The day before we were due to leave, we got a reply and went to see the little house in a quiet road behind Magdalene Street.

By mid-September we were living here.

[1] *Magna Tabula Glastonensis*, a history of the Abbey and its saints, now in the Bodleian Museum Oxford

On Bridie's Mound

Beckery is on the south-west outskirts of Glastonbury, in the shadow of Wearyall Hill. Today the area is dominated by big stores and light industrial yards, new estates and old streets of derelict warehouses. The Red Brick Building has been refurbished as a cultural hub. The Zig Zag is undergoing a DIY reclamation. A multi-million pound 'Beckery Bid' for regeneration funding is in the air. Then there's Morlands, the travellers' encampment close to the sewage works.

There's a history of antipathy between some locals and travellers: there were 'No Gypsies' signs here long before the Hippies came to town. The arrival of the 1980s New Age Travellers convoys caused further ructions. In February 2021 the Somerset News reported that 'The continued presence of an "illegal" encampment on a Glastonbury estate is risking "sinking a wonderful town into the abyss", according to concerned residents.'

The travellers lay claim to their ancient birthright: 'the land is ours'. They carry the lode – and the load – of a dark Earth Magic.

The name Beckery may derive from *Becc-Eriu* (Gaelic: 'Little Ireland') recalling the Irish hermits who formed a community here on what was then an island in the marshes. An excavation in 2016 uncovered the remains of what many archaeologists believe was the oldest monastic settlement in Britain. Some burials in the churchyard date back to the 5th century.

There was a chapel of St Mary Magdalene, which was later rededicated to St Brigid. Some claim it as the chapel in the Grail legend where Arthur has a vision of Our Lady serving the Child as the sacrament in the Mass. It's a disturbingly visceral glimpse into the mystery of transubstantiation, in which the bread and wine are literally changed into the body of Christ. In another version of the story, Our Lady gives Arthur a crystal cross, which he gifts to Glastonbury Abbey and has embossed on his shield.

The medieval historians William of Malmesbury and John of Glastonbury both record that St Brigid, also known as Brighid, Bridget, Brid, Bride or Bridie, stayed here for several years around 490 AD. This was the age of Celtic Christianity, when older, pagan elements were seamlessly integrated into the folk-religion of Ireland, Wales and the West of England.

The Irish saint Brigid or Bridie embodies many of the attributes of the pagan Goddess of that name. She is often depicted with a cow or a milking stool and performs little miracles – conjuring up an abundance of butter and even turning her bath-water into beer for a party of thirsty priests!

The Goddess was traditionally honoured with a fire festival held on 1st February. The name of her festival, Imbolc, derives from an Old Irish word meaning 'in the belly', a reference to the pregnant ewes at this time of year.

3rd February 2021. On Bridie's Mound. The wind flapping and raking the long grass. The shriek of a marsh bird. It's wild up here.

Katy makes a simple altar with sticks, dried flower petals, incense, a candle in a jar. We're about to perform an Imbolc ritual with Annabel, aka Autumn, and Chris, aka Sol Nigrum, keeper of the White Spring. Today's the astrological day of Imbolc. As we're about to begin, an astrologer and kombucha tea-brewer called Tom walks up the hill to join us, completing our unplanned pentagram. He affirms that we're beginning our ritual at the precise moment of the astrological Imbolc.

I ring the chimes and Annabel opens the ceremony, calling in Bridie in Her many forms. I speak the following invocation, which I've spoken at many Imbolc rituals. It invokes Bridie in three of Her aspects, as the Patron of Poets, Healers and Blacksmiths.

Imbolc

Bridie I am here
with my goose-feather quill
to trace the lucent songs of The Ancients.

Bridie I am here
with the chalice and snake
to receive and transmit your healing benediction.

Bridie I am here
with the bellows and tongs
to tend your holy fire of transformation.

Torism

For me, the spiritual quest is intimately connected with physical exertion – maybe it's my heathen spirit, or the shadow of an Old Puritan from a past life. Either way, I like to work it.

Since coming to live here, I often climb The Tor. It takes a great physical effort. For many years I've lived with asthma and emphysema – the result of a lifetime of smoking spliff. Only a year before I moved here, on a visit to Ireland, I'd gone down with a severe lung infection and spent a week gasping for breath.

My mind was bouncing around on The Astral. I had a lucid dream in which I wound up at a fairy orgy. My fairy wore a dress decorated with luminous globes. She plucked one off and popped it in my mouth. And everything changed. My strength returned. Of course the medical profession would never accept such anecdotal evidence but, yes – that night a fairy saved my life.

So climbing the Tor is a challenge. I have to stop at least seven times on the way up, lungs screaming for air, taking in the view as my breathing slowly calms. Onwards to the next way-station and a new perspective. Until at last, from the summit, the awesome panorama opens up.

You'll find seekers up here doing their thing to connect with the energies embodied in this astounding conical hill. Some will be performing rituals of their own devising to clear or activate the dragon lines. My friend Steve Radford spent hours switch-backing up the spiral maze which Geoffrey Russell believed would reveal The Secret of The Grail.[1] And why not?

Who knows? On our wanderings, we may stumble upon the secret portal to fairyland, The Chalice that holds Christ's blood, or the heathen cauldron that continually replenishes itself, feeding the body and illuminating the spirit. If we do, may we have the strength and wisdom to understand them and to work with them for the good of all – and be spared the delusion that we are the chosen one!

Personally, I don't expect to come across a literal chalice or cauldron. The Vision of the Grail is a poetic truth, born at the interface of mind and matter, where the human imagination discovers its deep connection with the Divine in all that lives – in every bird that sings, in the sun, the moon and the stars – the ineffable intelligence that dreams all this into being.

The conscious, rational left-brain seeks to analyse and deconstruct, reducing The Mysteries to things that can be placed in a particular Time or Place. Poetry speaks directly to the intuitive right-brain, pointing beyond the literal meaning of the words to the Unspeakable Mystery and its unfolding in our lives.

Self-transcendence is an essential element of the Spiritual Work. Yet the effort to transcend or even destroy the ego can perversely lead to self-obsession or a competitive approach to spiritual development. In our relentless quest for enlightenment, for life-changing visions and shamanic awakenings, we can lose sight of of the beauty and perfection right before our eyes.

So it's good to remind ourselves that Big Mind – empty enough to contain all this, every thought and deed of every fragile life-form – is already enlightened. On top of The Tor, looking out over the Somerset Levels and the hills, the Poldens and Mendips, the

Blackdown Hills and the distant Quantocks, sun going down in blushes and blazes of pure light, we may catch a glimpse – and, for one eternal moment, *Be It*.

In the light of which, all our many names for the Divine and our myriad paths to it are just 'delicious window-dressing' - and none the worse for that.

'The Goddess and The Green Man' is one of my favourite High Street shops servicing pagan pilgrims. During the dark days of the 2020-21 winter lockdown, I'd wander up the deserted High Street, gazing into the faery realms evoked in its exquisitely dressed window.

So here's one for all who climb and love The Tor: a spell of everyday enchantment.

[1] *The Secret of the Grail,* Geoffrey Russell, published in *Glastonbury A Study In Patterns (RILKO 1969)*

Sunset Over Avalon

Miracle enough:

this opalescent
cloud feathered sky-

mask; drifting
hexagons, dragon-

plumes; and the big boundless
blue

mind
peeping through;

emerald, violet, blood-
orange auras; February sun

and Full Moon on the water-
meadows, distant

mountains, or mist,
ensanguined. Christ’s

blood? Prismatic
tricks of the light?

Simply to see, to breathe, to be
this

sunset
over avalon,

this is the miracle
and the blessing,

the rest is just delicious
Goddess and Green Man

window-
dressing.

Full Moon, 27 February 2021

For centuries, Glastonbury Abbey, one of the great Christian centres in Europe, stood solitary in its 'Twelve Hides', land granted to Joseph of Arimathea by the pagan King Arviragus. By the 13th century a small town had sprung up around The Abbey, servicing the monks and catering for the pilgrims that thronged here. Following the 1539 sacking of The Abbey, Glastonbury reverted to being a sleepy Somerset village.

The Abbey grounds and ruins were bought by public subscription in 1907. They passed into the care of a Church of England Diocesan Trust, which commissioned Frederick Bligh Bond to conduct an archaeological survey. His exploratory work produced several remarkable finds, including the rediscovery of the Edgar Chapel to the east of the ruined church. In *The Gate of Remembrance*, published in 1918, he revealed that he had been guided by psychic messages received from 'The Company of Avalon' (conceived as the collective consciousness of The Abbey), a medieval monk named John Bryant and other spirit guides. The Trust was alarmed by these paranormal interventions and Bligh Bond was summarily dismissed, his reputation fatally damaged.

Bligh Bond's reliance on automatic writing may have been too much for the Church and the archaeological establishment. It was very much in tune with an upsurge of interest in the paranormal. The early 20th century was the age of Krishnamurti, Gurdjieff and Crowley, the Theosophists and The Golden Dawn.

Dion Fortune was one of the psychics working with Bligh Bond on the excavations at Glastonbury

Abbey, where she first established contact with spirit-entities she called 'The Watchers of Avalon'. She subsequently received instructions from the 'Ascended Masters' in trance states of what she termed 'inspirational mediumship'. Fortune established a retreat in Chalice Orchard, Well House Lane, and sought to promote a London-Glastonbury magical connection – with London as the 'head' and Glastonbury as the 'heart' of England.

The town's first great cultural and spiritual renaissance dates from this time. It was spearheaded by the composer Rutland Boughton and his librettist Reginald Buckley. Their Arthurian cycle of five operas and their best-known work *The Immortal Hour* drew on Celtic legends. Their aim was to do for Glastonbury what Richard Wagner had done for Bayreuth. Here they established England's first summer school of music and were the driving forces behind the Glastonbury Festivals held between 1914 and 1925.

Meanwhile, Alice Buckton had bought the Chalice Well to protect it for future generations. She established a pilgrims' hostel and an artistic community, reviving ancient crafts and producing many masques, pageants and plays. In 1922 she filmed a pageant in which local people acted out scenes from history and legend. That same year, the Rev. Lionel Smithett Lewis, the Vicar of Glastonbury, published *St Joseph of Arimathea at Glastonbury* reaffirming the founding legend of The Abbey.

It was in the wake of this creative revival that John Cowper Powys set his 1930s novel *A Glastonbury Romance*. Powys was not a Glastonbury resident, though he spent some of his youth in the area; his parents lived for many years in Montacute, Somerset.

The novel caused a scandal – and a libel action from the owner of the Wookey Hole Caves who thought one of its characters was based on him. Dion Fortune tartly observed that it 'has fluttered our local dove-cots to a painful extent. Do we behave like that in Glastonbury? I hadn't noticed it. I must have missed a lot.' [1]

I'd never even glanced at Powys' epic mystical novel, having wrongly assumed that it would be fey, affected, Tolkienesque. In fact it's closer to Hardy, setting its fleshy, earthy characters against the all-pervading myth of The Grail.

The novel's principle antagonists embody a conflict for the heart and soul of Glastonbury. Philip Crow strives to turn it into an industrial town. He already owns a dye-works and hopes to revive tin-mining up in the Wookey Hole caves. The plan includes building a new road through the Somerset Levels and replacing the 'Pomparles' bridge over the River Brue. His adversary is John Geard, a charismatic Christian healer and Mayor of Glastonbury, with a vision to restore the town to its ancient glory as a place of pilgrimage.

Crow and Geard represent the struggle between materialism and mysticism, part of what Powys conceives as a primordial battle between the heathen gods and the Christian mysteries that have taken root in Glastonbury. The conflict is enacted in the lives of his huge cast of characters, all of whom to some extent embody the dualism that Powys sees as rooted in the Prime Cause of Being.

His great achievement is to ground The Grail and the unfolding of its Mysteries in the day-to-day life of Glastonbury. And not only in its people – every animal, bird, even the lowliest wood louse plays its part in the integrated conscious life of this particular place. The novel also conceives of the Glastonbury Watchers, spiritual entities that keep watch over the unfolding of all that happens here, just as the vicar and his son Sam observe the fish in their aquarium.

I first met Paul Weston, psychographer and author, at 11am on 28th November 2020 in the Edgar Chapel at the east end of the Abbey ruins. I was hosting an informal celebration of William Blake's Birthday. Seven Blakeans showed up. Paul was first to arrive. I'd heard that he'd previously organised a Blake festival in Glastonbury and was anxious not to step on his toes.

We soon discover we share not only a love of Blake and the Divine Feminine, but ways of seeing connections and patterns. We exchange copies of our own books and Paul recommends *A Glastonbury Romance* as the best introduction to what he calls 'Deep Glastonbury'. He also warns me that I'm in it!

The ambivalent protagonist of this novel, written before I was born, is John Crow, a charismatic yet disreputable trickster showman. He even has the cheek to put on a blasphemous modern Mystery Play – just as *my* John Crow had done in 2000 and 2010 in Southwark. I'd done all that in blissful ignorance of my literary namesake, and I wasn't inclined to attempt to repeat it here in Glastonbury.

Nevertheless, reading about a character who shares my name and at least some characteristics was unnerving, especially when 'Mad Bet' becomes obsessed with John Crow and decides that if she can't have him no one else will. One night, up on The Tor...

Suffice to say it held me spellbound throughout January 2021, and that it gave me pause for thought. Paul had the idea that someone in town should be reading the novel at noon on the 5th March. I'd playfully suggested a 'Crow's Day' along the lines of Dublin's Bloom's Day. Given the then draconian measures against public gatherings, we agreed not to publicise this one and that only he and I should meet.

We convened once more in the ruins of the Edgar Chapel unearthed by Bligh Bond. I deferred to him as to the form our Powys celebration would take. He insisted that I choose which passages to read.

I began with the opening paragraph: 'At the striking of noon on a certain 5th of March...' [2]

Then a passage on how 'the whole of John Crow's life was a sequence of "other sides" - "other sides" of roads, "other sides" of thoughts, "other sides" of ideas, religions, labours, activities…' [3]

We closed with Sam Dekker's vision of The Grail with a shining fish swimming in its depths, an '*Ichthus* out of the Absolute'.[4] The fish symbol was used by the early Christians, and often incorporated the acrostic 'ICHTHUS' formed by the initials of the Greek words meaning: 'Jesus Christ Son of God Saviour'. We read this passage by the entrance to Our Lady's Chapel, which is geometrically proportioned to represent the fish-shaped *Vesica Piscis*.

[1] Dion Fortune, *Avalon of the Heart*

[2] John Cowper Powys, *A Glastonbury Romance*

[3] Powys, *A Glastonbury Romance*

[4] Powys, *A Glastonbury Romance*

The Iron Age Lake Village

The Somerset Levels are an expanse of wetland meadows and marshes to the west of Glastonbury. Before the construction of dykes along the Bristol Channel, at high tide The Levels were regularly inundated with brackish water.

An intricate system of ditches, or rhynes, has since drained and reclaimed the land, where sheep and cattle now graze. In winter there are epic murmurations over Ham Wall, with thousands upon thousands of starlings sky-writing then plummeting down into the reed beds. By spring the lush grasslands are bright with golden buttercups.

The entire area is below sea-level. The apocalyptic final chapter of John Cowper Powys' *A Glastonbury Romance* draws on folk-memories of flood. Dion Fortune met an old woman whose grandmother could remember the water lapping at St Benignus Church.[1] Those flood-waters would have been uncomfortably close to our house! During heavy rains The Levels are still prone to flooding. When the evening mists well up it's easy to imagine The Isle of Avalon rising out of a lake.

So the idea of Joseph of Arimathea sailing up the swollen River Brue to land at the foot of Wearyall Hill is at least plausible. The river delta was navigable at high tide, opening trade routes with the Severn Estuary and the wider world. Some say Joseph was a tin merchant, and that on a previous trip he'd brought his nephew Jesus, to show him the world and introduce him to the Druid Mysteries. There's a Somerset saying: 'As sure as Our Lord walked at Priddy' and a folk-song

Joseph was a tin man. French folk-religion has its own legends of visits by Jesus and Mary Magdalene – who's to say they didn't come here too?

The earliest extant record of Joseph's coming to Glastonbury is a 13th century annotation in the margin of William of Malmesbury's history. (Both William and John of Glastonbury refer to older lost texts and to books in The Abbey's world-famous library.) We do know that, a century before Joseph of Arimathea's supposed visit, our ancestors were living out here in the marshes, in what has become known as the Glastonbury Lake Village.

The Iron Age village was not literally in a lake; more a swamp, with the channels of River Brue winding through it towards the sea. The village was raised on piles, surrounded by a defensive stockade and accessed by causeways or by dugout canoe. Being in a swamp offered a measure of protection from hostile intruders. The wetland habitat attracted birds and fish, providing a plentiful source of food.

The Lake Village was occupied for two hundred years, from 250 to 50 BC. At any one time there were up to fourteen round houses built of hazel and willow and thatched with reeds. The villagers made tools, ladders, wheels, baskets, bowls and other utensils, even gaming dice. They worked metals and created decorative pots, adorned themselves with jewellery, pins, rings and glass beads, looked at themselves in mirrors. We don't know what they believed or what it was like to be them, but we know enough to recognise something of ourselves in them.

We know all this because in 1892 Arthur Bulleid, a local medical student and antiquarian,was drawn to investigate several hummocks in the fields near Godley. From then through to 1907 he worked with Harold St George Gray of the Somerset Archaeology and Natural History Museum. Their excavations uncovered the footprint and foundations of the Iron Age village, a dugout canoe, and the tools and artefacts described above, the evidence on which we can reconstruct a world of two thousand years ago.

Is it important to distinguish fact from fiction, history from myth? As a rule, yes. Being able to differentiate qualities and properties is intrinsic to our survival and prosperity. For a witch or wizard, discernment is a crucial faculty. If we blur such distinctions our magical thinking can easily slide into delusion. We've seen how during the Plague Year some New Agers retreated into zealotry, refusing to engage with evidence-based research, much as fanatical Christian Creationists reject evidence that The Earth is more than six thousand years old.

The site of the Iron Age village is in the fields between Godney Road and Great Withy Drove. The artefacts were removed during the original early 20th century excavation, and the foundations of the village have been reburied to protect them from the elements.

On my first attempt to visit the site, I walked along Dyehouse Lane north towards Godney Road. Just after where the road wiggles over a little bridge, I mistakenly branched left along the public footpath through the fields. An hour later, I found myself walking a track between dead brushwood groves, my skin prickling with the sense of ancient lives, other worlds. It was like slipping through a wormhole in time. What follows is my report.

Sometimes you have to get lost to get found.

[1] Dion Fortune, *Avalon of the Heart*

School Trip

when we entered the village
they were wary.

in the marshes, strangers
may come to rob or worse.

we couldn't speak
their language. we

didn't know what to do so
we sang them a song.

and one, then all start laughing.
one bangs a drum.

and suddenly we all know
what's to be done.

Teacher
reminds us
that if Mum and Dad
had not come together...

- Sex, Miss?
Ew! Gross!

yes, children, and if
your Grand- and Great-
and Great-Great-Grand-
Ma and Pa tracking back

across millennia
hadn’t met and mated,
we wouldn’t be here
to wonder.

exchanged gifts: gave them a 12-inch
classic dub track; their Chief
still wears the vinyl breastplate.

they gave us pottery shards, a pouch
of dried bird bones and
something we couldn’t quite place.

then home through the lush
meadow, by the green
scummy rhyne.

a stand of yellow willow
skirting the river,
lit up in a fan of sunbeams.

before us
the spiral track coils up
The Tor:

the serpent;
the egg.

so then we had to write it up
in our own words, and these are mine:

it’s one thing
to have seen and for one moment, been
                    the very thing we seek.

it’s another to bring it all
back home, ground it in this world

                    so

unborn generations will one day
come to know and, knowing,
                    long to go

                    on a school trip

to the Iron Age
Lake Village.

Out Of It

When the Glastonbury energy vortex gets too much, sanctuary is near. The water-meadows, the wooded hummocks, the hills… Walk down Stone Down Lane to the Gog and Magog Oaks and the remnants of an ancient Druid grove.

Katy and I drove south to Compton Dundon, to sit inside the hollow trunk of a thousand year old yew tree in the churchyard and see the sun light up Lollover Hill. To the ruined Muchelney Abbey, blackberrying. Over the rolling hills to Somerton for cream-tea in the Market Place or dinner in The White Hart garden. To the River Parrett at Langport, or for a chancy wild dip in the River Brue by the stone bridge at East Lydford.

We tracked the St Michael line south west to St Michael's Church at Othery and on to Burrowbridge and The Mump, a conical hump like The Tor with the ruin of (yet another) St Michael's church on its summit stark against the winter sky.

West along the narrow lanes of The Somerset Levels – Meare, Westhay, Burtle. To the marshes at Ham Wall to witness murmurations of starlings, then walk the Sweet Track. On Holywell Road beyond Shapwick we paid homage to the abandoned holy well, and at Chilton Polden we chanced on a Goose Lane!

North – Wells, Wookey. Burnham-on-Sea on a gusty winter's day, the beach deserted save only for the dust-devils dancing by the cliffs. 'As sure as Our Lord walked at Priddy' we walked the Nine Barrows. And on to the otherworldly landscapes of Velvet Bottom, the mounds and hollows shaped by lead-mines since Roman times, the hedgerows a mist of bluebells.

One bright sunny day in mid-March we headed up into the Quantock Hills on the Somerset-North Devon border. It's inspiring country for a poet to take a walking holiday, which is how in 1797 Samuel Taylor Coleridge came to write *Kubla Khan*, one of the most evocative poems in the English language. He was returning from Lynton to his cottage in Nether Stowey when he was taken ill. On the poem's original manuscript he wrote that it was composed:

… in a sort of Reverie brought on by two grains of Opium taken to check a dysentery, at a Farm House between Porlock & Linton.

In the preface to the 1816 printed poem, he claims he dreamed the entire poem. On waking, he wrote it down in a burst of creativity. But then 'he was unfortunately called out by a person on business from Porlock'. The interruption effectively dispelled his visionary trance. The unfortunate 'person from Porlock' has become a literary trope, emblematic of those who intrude on the creative process with their petty concerns, disrupting the genius at work.

Coleridge was a regular user of opium, and an enthusiastic participant in Dr Humphrey Davy's experiments with nitrous oxide at the Bristol Pneumatic Institution.

Around Glastonbury you'll see people off their faces on acid or ketamine or some new consciousness-expanding drug. They may look lost, stupid or lairy. They may nevertheless be undergoing a profound and potentially life-changing experience. Let's take care not to Porlock their inner space, where Coleridge and Taliesin drink at the font.[1]

[1] I thought about including a separate meditation *On Drugs*. Specifically on the intelligent use of psychedelic sacraments, which I've used over fifty years as catalysts and tools in my spiritual practice. The Goose visions were initially triggered by huge doses of LSD, and many of the early Cross Bones rituals were conducted in an altered state. I've been fortunate, or maybe I'm someone who takes naturally to psychedelics, being neurologically disposed to surrender and trust the force. I've also seen many casualties, people who crashed and burned or spiralled into delusion and psychosis. To responsibly engage with all these complexities and contradictions – well, that's a whole other book. So I'll keep this to a simple footnote. I wouldn't advise *anyone* to follow my example – or to take *anything*. If you do, get it from a trusted source and take care of your 'set and setting'. Be in a relaxed, receptive state of mind, in a place you feel safe and not likely to be disturbed. There's nothing quite like tripping in nature, though you may have to deal with unexpected intrusions from the physical world and its inhabitants. You don't need drugs to journey to The Otherworlds. Meditation, breath-work, visualisation, chanting, drumming and dancing are just some of the ways by which practitioners can access altered states. Howsoever you travel, the practice of shining emptiness and non-attachment will see you through whatever state you find yourself in.

Xanadu #2: The Quantock Quantum

In a parallel Dreamtime of his own devising
Sam remembers to put a sign on the farmhouse door:

BEWARE	BEWARE
flashing eyes	floating hair

Having recently drunk The Milk of Paradise
Mr S.T.C. is presently building domes in air
with music and song to reconfigure
Poetry Forever!

NO PERSONS FROM PORLOCK PLEASE!

The New John of Glastonbury

John of Glastonbury was the 14th century chronicler of The Abbey who placed Joseph of Arimathea at the heart of its founding legend. In the 1970s John Michell was a key player in Glastonbury's revival, creating a body of work that informed the spiritual world-view of the counter-culture. At the 1971 Glastonbury Festival he advised on the construction of the Pyramid Stage, based on the dimensions of the Great Pyramid.

John came here when working on his first book *The Flying Saucer Vision*. He later recalled travelling in horse-drawn carts with the musician Mark Palmer and friends, camping near The Tor and seeing dancing lights in the sky above St Michael's tower, which was by then famous for UFO sightings.

His next book *The View Over Atlantis* had an entire chapter on Glastonbury, summarising its ancient legends and its early 20th century renaissance. He placed it at the heart of his vision of a world-wide network of ley-lines or 'dragon lines' channelling the Earth's energetic currents. His insights shaped my own intuitive connection with the town and the land.[1]

I first met John briefly in the early 1980s. He was a close friend and long-time lover of my friend Evelyn, an underground film-maker and esoteric networker from New York. I was performing in one of Ev's improvised video-shoots, filmed in the squatted Cambodian Embassy. John was hanging around and I made clumsy attempts to engage him in conversation. He was patient, gracious, charming.

During the all-night shoots most of us we were tripping. At one point I was persuaded to get into a heavy bear-suit. It was hot and suffocating. I briefly collapsed and a beautiful woman called Louise came and eased me out of it. The experience of being stripped of a bestial skin to human nakedness was like an atavistic ritual; it was also intensely erotic.

A few days later I visited her at John's flat in Powis Gardens, Notting Hill, the walls lined with home-made bookcases stacked with old tomes. He wasn't there, and we ended up having a night of passion on the bare floor-boards. Afterwards, when it had fully sunk in that they were also lovers, I felt guilty, as if I'd shabbily disrespected John's hospitality. Louise assured me that they had a very open relationship. (John often had several on the go.) Nevertheless, although the sex was great and Louise and I are still good friends, we never did it again. Nor did I ever mention it to John.

One day I bumped into him on Hampstead Heath, sprawled under a tree, rolling spliffs with the crumbs of hashish he used to carry loose in his jacket pockets. Every so often excited blokes would run over to announce: 'I think we've found another one!' John was directing a group of enthusiastic ley-hunters. He'd gravely examine the line on a map, purse his lips and pronounce: 'That certainly looks promising!' As one such hunter scurried off, John added, with a wry smile: 'You have to encourage them!'

In the 1990s, our mutual friend (and hash dealer) Ev often used to invite us both to her Council flat in Camden, where we'd spend many a happy afternoon free-ranging from metaphysics to gossip. He liked to riff on Plato, saying that once someone has the *idea* that something exists, it will eventually be proved to exist. He argued that reductionist materialism and scientific empiricism are themselves belief-systems, models of reality constructed to justify their own 'proofs'. John was convinced that, in medieval times, people believed in Angels and therefore saw them and spoke with them – on hills, by rivers, even in London streets as William Blake did.

One afternoon, we continued the conversation as we walked up the hill to the tube. I'll never forget standing underground in the Swiss Cottage ticket hall, spellbound, as John evoked images of Angels constructing their Sacred Architectures in and beyond the material world.

Hash. John loved his hash. And acid. Some of his best ideas came to him when tripping or toking late into the night in Powis Gardens. Like Keats, he saw that if an idea was beautiful, it was probably true.

John's use of mind-altering substances don't invalidate the visionary insights they inspired – though we can't always trust his maths or his maps! It does makes me smile to hear him sometimes cited in scholarly works as if he were some dry academic poring over ancient manuscripts in the British Museum!

In his later years, John was drawn back to Glastonbury. Before he died, he married Denny, the popular Archdruidess who was later elected Mayor of Glastonbury. I don't know if Evelyn ever crossed swords with Denny – as she did with other rivals for John's affection. She once came to Glastonbury for a dinner in his honour and spent a miserable night in The George and Pilgrim feeling lonely and abandoned.

John's marriage to Denny, which lasted only months, shocked his family and his London friends. (I subsequently learned that Denny had been deeply hurt by their rejection of her.) To Ev, who'd thought of herself as his significant other, the news was devastating, though they remained close to the end. We attended his memorial service, sharing a laugh when son Jason, who only got to meet his errant father as a grown man, told of John smuggling his personal stash of hash on their first foreign holiday.

After his death, Ev seemed to lose the will to live. She started giving away possessions, getting ready for her own departure. In what seemed like no time at all, she too was gone.

I inherited some of her books, including a few that John had given her. After I moved to Glastonbury, I reread the posthumously published *Michellany,* a collection of tributes by friends interleaved with essays by John. Here, he describes his own first trip to Glastonbury in 1966, with the poet Harry Fainlight:

Glastonbury… was quite different from how it is today. The New Age had not yet dawned there… no health foods, no weird-looking people on the streets. Surly publicans were not yet displaying "No Hippy" placards. Instead, the signs on their doors said "No Gypsies." [2]

They ate at The Abbey Cafe, a greasy spoon in Benedict Street, where they unnerved a lorry driver by talking about UFOs. They befriended the owner Gino, and John subsequently painted a mural on the cafe wall. It depicted the St Michael dragon-line as the spine of Blake's 'Giant Albion'. The line links The Tor with The

Mump at Burrowbridge and a series of mounds associated with St Michael churches, extending west to St Michael's Mount in Cornwall and east to Avebury and beyond. Along the line, John painted a pair of intertwining serpents, creating a caduceus. He was intuitively drawing on William Stukeley's 1743 book which identified Avebury as 'a winged serpent temple'. His ideas would inspire and reverberate through an entire corpus of Earth Mysteries, in which the mercurial dragon-currents of the Michael and Mary Lines spiral around a unifying spine.

The penultimate photograph in *Michellany* is of John's last journey, his mortal remains borne on Mark Palmer's horse-drawn cart with the sign on the back: GENERAL DEALER. When I look at it I see John in Eternity, eyes twinkling with mischief.

From the room where I write this I look out on St Benedict's (Benignus) Church where John and Denny were married. It's aligned with The Abbey and Stonehenge on the Dod Line, another of his mercurial spirit-paths. A living reminder of how John influenced my own journey, enabling me find my place in the mythic landscape he helped create.

[1] see also *City of Revelation: On the Proportions and Symbolic Numbers of the Cosmic Temple* (1972) and *New Light On The Ancient Mystery of Glastonbury* (1990) John Michell

[2] *Glastonbury: The First Encounter,* John Michell, published in *Michellany,* 2010. First published as a review of *The Sun and The Serpent* by Paul Broadhurst and Hamish Miller, 2010

Snakes

Hero,
Knight of the Kaos
Konvoy, Jack-the-
Lad of Beanfield legend.
Rogue druid, Taurean, trouble-
maker and all round good egg.

We met backstage at The Warp
Party in The Drome
caverns under London Bridge, 1999. You
were the bearded man in the strapless pink
PVC dress. Brothers in Light we sailed
the psychedelic underworld, all through the night
and into the day, the party that never sleeps,
bonding as our parents once did
in their wars, waging Peace
and Love on all comers.

Hadn't seen you in fifteen years.
but when you've been through The Warp
you're kin. You were tickled
when Katy and I moved to Glastonbury.
Three times we trekked out to the camp
at Morlands, between Bridie's Mound
and the Sewage Works, on the edge
of everything. You weren't in.
But we spoke on the phone and it was like
old times. Spoke of age and its privations,
our dwindling band of Elders,
our close shaves and miracle cures.

Anette broke the news, in shock
though she'd seen your decline. Picked us up
in her cart drawn by the mighty shire horse
Bear. We processed up the High Street
like shabby royalty. On Chalice Hill, Bear
broke into a trot. The sun was out. The sky was blue.
And as the Tor hove into view
you were with us and we
were there with you.

Anette asked us to conduct the ceremony –
as much as anyone could conduct that freebooting
rabble of crusty sprites – in Beckery, where alchemy
is worked raw-knuckled. We gather
in a mucky horseshoe
in the horses' paddock-cum-
cremation ground. Your proper job
Traveller's send-off. Craig pipes us in.

Solomon, your eldest, seizes the mosh-pit
to kick off with your sign-off, last night at The Warp:
You've all got
the rest of your lives off!

Anette tells the one about how you got banned
from Stonehenge for taking on site-security:
What's this? Turnstiles?
This isn't a licensed nightclub!

Pok does your elegy. I do *I Am The Wind* with
I am the Grace that transfigures the Sin.
I am the Wound that prefigures the Healing.
I am the Light at the Travellers' Inn.

It was ragged and noisy and
some of the congregation fell over
in the mud. It was true to you, Snakes,
all you were and ever are.

Paul used your old Snake stick to ignite
the kerosene-soaked cremation cart and

WHOOOSH!

Around the charred skeletal chassis
and lattice, some saw the scorched
shadow of a Viking longboat. I see you
in the *vesica piscis*, the chalice of the fish.

Trust you've already overturned a few
apple-carts, in that part of heaven
reserved for outlaws, where they play
old-skool acid house in all-night chai-tents.

I see you, Snakes, glide
and bask in grass and meadow-sweet.
I see you, freak, god-man, astride
Anette's shire horse, Aslan, who went before.

Open pathways, my brother, my friend,
on your free ride

into the Sun.

Snakes' funeral
Morland's Travellers' site, Beckery
Friday 26th March 2021

In The Garden

In September 2020, the night after we'd moved into our new home, I wrote:

Today we saw the most vivid rainbow of our lives, spanning the tower of St John's Church and the Tor, framing us in the garden, laughing like kids. Sparrows sing in the pyracantha bush, feeding greedily on the orange berries. We've inherited three goldfish in a garden pond, which I feed as a daily meditation. And last night Katy heard an owl and met a toad. Auspicious omens.

We fell in love with our new home the moment we saw the garden, with its cherry tree, pond and fat Buddha sat under an arching pyracantha (firethorn) bush. By the time we moved in, the bush was golden with berries. Every day the sparrows flitted down from their nests to feed. We communed with them all through the winter and into the spring. They sang their songs and I wrote two for them.

The sparrows were our teachers. Like the bells of St John the Baptist marking the hours and quarter-hours, they taught us to slow down and be fully present in the Here and Now.

England's finest nature poet has no known connection with Glastonbury, except that the sparrows appear to have conjured up his spirit in our garden. The spell was all but complete when he made his surprise appearance, to be blessed.

The Soul of Mad John Clare

Spring coils... and springs
in a whirr of sparrow wings.

The sparrows flit and poke and push
In the pyracantha bush;

The orange berries all but gone.
Fat sparrows chortle in the sun.

Vision of joy and strength and health,
Of Life in love with Life itself.

And in this moment, I, the sky
And all the birds that in me fly...

I bless the light, the sky, the air.
I bless the soul of mad John Clare.

Brazen in the fire-thorn,
Sparrows to their Eden born.

Grubbing in the lush green leaves
To feed the hatchlings in the eaves.

Above them, in the shifting light,
Ravens, doves switch paths in flight.

Higher still, marauding crows
Dive-bomb a flock of wayward gulls.

After the final, parting ‘crawk’...
The silent, circling sparrow-hawk.

Sparrows, fly free, but please take care.
It’s not all Peace and Love up there.

31/03/2021

The Book of Sparrow

Sparrows don't have to be taught:
'Be what thou art, not what thou ought!'

Easter

Sunday, wearily on Wearyall
Hill, King Fisherman

Waters old Tom's mouldering
Corpse. 'Sprouted? Has it?'

Black dog sharpens
His claw.

And this is what we're all here
Waiting for. Renewal.

One vision, one Act to heal the Earth
And us all in it together.

After The Plague and The Age of Opinion…
Out of Division...

Nature's act of grace – implacable,
Indifferent to bones picked –

Thorn buds open;
Blackbirds sing;

And it's Spring.

Stone Down Lane

April burgeons to St George,
waking the Dragon line

in riotous pageant: dandelion,
daisy and buttery celandine.

Blushing linnet
chirrups in the hedgerow.

‘How do you know
it’s a linnet, crow?’

‘Linnet told me so,
and so I believe,

as when I answer to crow
I do not deceive.’

May Day

A key part of the modern reinvention of paganism was the establishment of a Wheel of the Year with eight solar festivals – the solstices, equinoxes and, between them, the four cross-quarters: Imbolc, Beltane, Lughnasadh or Lammas, and Samhain (Hallowe'en). There's little evidence that our native ancestors observed such a formal unified ritual calendar; diverse Celtic tribes had their own seasonal rituals, which contemporary Wiccans and pagans adopted and adapted to form the 'Wheel'.

The May Day Beltane celebration has become an important event in the Glastonbury calendar. Goddess devotees spend weeks preparing, the men hewing the phallic maypole, the women shaping the earth to receive it in a hand-worked yoni. There are Dragon processions down the High Street, with singing and dancing and celebrants done up in all manner of ceremonial fancy dress.

On May 1st 2021, due to the ongoing restrictions, celebrations were muted. There was the sense that it was all happening secretly, with random outbreaks of illicit carousing. I was out and about early to welcome in the summer with a lusty rendition of *Hal and Tow*. It was my first public performance in over a year and I felt a bit self-conscious. The crowds on Magdalene Street were encouraging. A man called Timmy asked if he could play my bodhran. He then accompanied me as I did my *Hail The Queen of the May (Beltane)* with everyone joining in on the refrain.

By mid-morning I'd worked my way up the hill. Outside St John's church I teamed up with my old friend Pok the Bard who read from his recently published *Book of Bok*. I sang my other *Queen of the May* song, the one I wrote for Katy, and the first ever performance of *Sing, Sing The Fisher King*.

We bimble back down the hill to join the poets and musicians on the sound system at the Market Cross. I know the MC, Ash, from the festival poets' fire-circles. He'd often credited me as an influence on his development as a Bardic poet. I respect his hell fire raps ablaze with righteous Old Time Gnostic Religion. Ash is a Contrarian. We last fell out when he took umbrage at my playful suggestion that he change his name from Ash the Destroyer to Ash the Mender.

Today, all is forgiven. We're delighted to see one another. He gets me in the show with a generous introduction. I cast *A Little Spell of Unforgetting*, the first of my new Glastonbury spells, and a participatory version of *Hail The Queen of the May (Beltane)*.

In the late afternoon we head over to the field adjoining Stone Down Lane at the back of the Tor, where revellers have erected a maypole, to share more Bardic offerings.

The performance of old spells and incantations in specific settings is an integral part of my work to introduce The Goose Spirit to the spirits of Avalon and to reaffirm the London-Glastonbury connection. I end the day with a third recitation of the invocation I always make on May Day for The true Queen.

Hail!

Beltane

Now in the beat of the turning year,
Our work is to play
And rejoice in being here.
Hail The Queen of The May!

Now let the drums beat
On this her Holy Day.
Sing and dance in the street.
Hail The Queen of The May!

Earth, Water, Fire and Air
Round the May-pole weave your way.
Red ribbons in her hair.
Hail The Queen of The May!

Queen of the wanton and wild:
Here in the lovers at play.
Here in the heart of the child
Hail The Queen of The May!

Here the goddess and her god
Frolic and sport and play.
And we follow where their hooves have trod.

Shhh…

Magdalene Street

On Magdalene Street
Where two Marys meet,
The Apostles' Apostle
And The Mother of God.

They meet and they greet
On Magdalene Street
With a hug and a kiss
And a knowing nod.

On Magdalene Street
To Her Beltane drum beat
The Goddess is frisky.
She's up for The Rod.

On Magdalene Street
Where many ways meet
This is not sacrilegious.

It's not even odd.

The Body on The Hill

My poem *Easter*, written on Easter Sunday 4th April, references The Fisher King on Wearyall Hill and lines from T. S. Eliot's *The Waste Land* which ask whether a corpse has sprouted or will bloom and warn of the Dog that will 'dig it up again'.

On Saturday 22nd May, just before Whitsun, Paul Weston sends me the news of a body found on Wearyall Hill. The Police believe it's the mortal remains of Lawrence Kemp, who disappeared last August. I remember seeing his face on the MISSING posters on lampposts when we first moved here. Paul writes:

There are multiple nuances in the airwaves that I'm currently processing but the most obvious and extremely grim one is the motif of hidden putrefaction it shares with the 2003 'maggot murder'. I reckon you are perhaps a poet laureate of Glasto now and the muse may force you into eventually producing a contemplation of this deep manifestation.

Those posters had said that Lawrence was last seen on August 1st, Lammas. His decomposing body must have lain in the woods up on Wearyall Hill nearly ten months; many have expressed amazement that it was never found, given that the Hill is much visited and popular with dog-walkers.

The 'maggot murder' was committed in August 2003, when Keith Newnham stabbed his friend James MacFarlane, leaving his corpse to rot. Paul connects this with repeated acts of mutilation inflicted on the

Holy Thorn tree and with neolithic rites that seem to be re-enacting themselves in the lives of the travellers living around Wearyall Hill, much as the old myths reinvent themselves in the John Cowper Powys novel.

I'm not sure I'd claim or even want to be a 'Glasto laureate', but I'm grateful to Paul for regularly seeding my imagination with his discoveries and insights. I reply to his message, enclosing a copy of my previous *Easter* poem, which may seem to have intuited the existence of a corpse up on Wearyall Hill.

Like each of Glastonbury's four hills, Wearyall embodies its own myth. Tour guides like to tell how Joseph of Arimathea led his disciples up over the hill, declaring: 'We are weary all.' (Locals call it Wirral Hill, which suggests an entirely different derivation.) As Joseph thrust his staff into the earth; it rooted and blossomed. The Glastonbury Thorn is of a genus found in the Middle East. It has the distinction of flowering twice a year, at Christmas and Easter. Every Christmas a sprig of blossom is gifted to The Queen and traditionally adorns her dinner-table. Cuttings of The Holy Thorn can be seen in the churchyards of St John's, St Benedict's and The Abbey; a scion of the original grew on Wearyall Hill. It attracted reverence and devotion, and was transformed into a 'cloutie' or prayer tree, its branches hung with ribbons. However, it was also the victim of repeated acts of desecration, and in December 2019 it was brutally hacked down.

Wearyall Hill is believed by some to be the site of The Fisher King's castle, where The Grail is kept. Dion Fortune, who called it The Isle of The Holy Thorn, claimed it was a place of initiation, the centre of a Mystery Cult.

In his *Glastonbury Psychogeography* book, Paul Weston relates the psychic traumas unleashed by the decapitation of The Holy Thorn, which he links with a scene from *A Glastonbury Romance:*

… when one night a character intuited that there were forces in the air that sought to 'murder the Grail'.

In the Powys novel, it was on Wearyall Hill that my namesake John Crow had his fateful meeting with Mad Bet on a wild stormy Maundy Thursday night with madness and murder in the air.

On Tuesday 25th May, Paul and I meet by chance at our magic place, the Edgar Chapel in the Abbey ruins. Whilst sensitive to the human tragedy of Lawrence's death, Paul is still brooding on its dark mythic resonances. In 1921, exactly a century before the discovery of the body, Dion Fortune had began working with Bligh Bond and had experienced her first psychic contacts which prefigured the Avalonian revival.

A month or so after our meeting in The Abbey, I wrote *Human Rites*, evoking an archaic funeral rite in which the putrefaction of the body nurtures the flowering of new life. I see that this too carries echoes and resonances of Lawrence's tragic death. I can't explain how my intuitive writing may have made connections between this personal tragedy and the unfolding of what Paul calls 'Deep Glastonbury'.

I can say that neither of these two poems was consciously alluding to the finding of the body. I didn't know Lawrence, though the memory of his sad, sensitive face on the poster still haunts me. I asked around and found out he'd lodged for a time with my friends Liz and Trev[1]. They said he was a sweet man, happiest when working on his bicycle in the back yard, seemingly living in his own world but not obviously suffering from mental health or addiction problems. A gentle, kind, vulnerable man who somehow slipped through the safety nets that catch us when we fall.

'There but for the Grace…'

Open pathways, Lawrence.

The following poem has no hidden meanings. It simply describes a physical event and a spirited exchange! It's here to lighten things up.

[1] Williams and Jones, writer and magical gardener, founders of The Glastonbury Occult Conference, owners of the Witchcraft shop and former keepers of esoteric shops around town, including the much-missed Cat and Cauldron close to The Abbey Gate.

On Wearyall Hill

Dodgy tattooed geezer swaggers
down Hill Head tossing a chrome hub-cap
in the air, to catch or let fall, clang and clatter.

As we pass, trading edgy grins, he says:
‘One of these days it’s going to come
down and hit me on the head.’

And I, like the Christian-animist Avalon
evangelist I am, reply: ‘When it do, Brother,
may you see the Light!’

Summer Solstice & St John's Eve

In the days leading up to the Summer Solstice, Glastonbury throngs with visiting sun-worshippers, their faces emblazoned with glittering solar-inspired make-up. The lifting of pandemic restrictions has been delayed again, and there's rain on the way, but that isn't about to stop the pagan pilgrimage.

'Solstice', literally 'sun standing still', refers to the days on either side of the longest day and shortest night (contrariwise for the Winter Solstice) when the sun appears to pause on its passage through the heavens. Now that we no longer conceive Earth as the centre of the Universe, with stars, suns and planets revolving around it, we see that the Earth orbits the Sun and that the changes in daylight are caused by its curvature and the angle of its axis. Still, there's much to be said for the primitive vision, the poetic truth that envisions the sun's journey through the empyrean that enfolds us.

Students of the Earth Mysteries often conceive of The Tor as an accumulator for the reception and distribution of dragon energy. They envision the spark of the rising Sun striking the mound to ignite and activate the Earth currents. Dion Fortune visualised a circle of stones atop The Tor, an ancient, open Temple of the Sun. It's easy to imagine our Neolithic ancestors ascending the hill in a spiral procession, banging drums, lighting a fire on the summit and conducting a ceremony to greet the dawn.

Contemporary New Age and pagan revellers try to recreate the feel of those ancient ceremonies, freely borrowing from indigenous cultures. As the sun rises,

‘Grandfather Fire’ flares and flickers in the fire-pit. A robed priestess solemnly intones an invocation and blessing, thoughtfully including those indigenous peoples, many of whom now live increasingly marginalised lives. Other priestesses stand guard, clutching their shaman’s drums, primed to affirm the benediction. Then the drummers kick in and the hill-top ritual reverts to a joyful, exuberant rave.

I wasn’t there. Many times I’ve gone through the night at Stonehenge waiting for that first ray of the rising sun to rise behind the Hele Stone. Since living in Glastonbury I’ve climbed The Tor at least once a week and witnessed some truly awesome sunsets. As the longest day neared, I entertained the idea of getting up at 3am for the trek through town and up the steep hill for my first Glastonbury summer solstice sunrise.

Forecasts of an overcast sky and patchy rain made me think twice. And the day before I met Tim Raven, the charming harpist I’d befriended during my Beltane revels. Since then we’d often met in the High Street and I’d joined some of his impromptu jams in the courtyard of Cafe Sol. I’d done a poem accompanied by Tim on harp – which had completely transported a visiting healer! I ask Tim if he’s heading up The Tor for Solstice. He’s decided not to:

‘I wanted to get up there and make some real ‘fairy music’. But once those drummers start up...’

And I remember how many a chilled-out festie had been rudely interrupted by young men (generally men, usually white and often dread-locked) banging on huge djembes which they hadn’t learned to play. It’s not just the din they make. It’s the testosterone-fuelled monkey-mind energy the drums seem to unleash in them, driving them to fill in every available beat!

So I was in two minds whether to see in the solstice on The Tor. And two minds is never a good place to plant a ritual observance.

Later I watched a video filmed on The Tor just after sunrise, which is how I know about those robed priestesses. The drummers weren't as dreadful as I'd feared; they just about held a solid beat that everyone could shake to. Bless them, and all beings.

Communal acts of worship are all too rare in an Age of individualistic belief-systems, and worth cherishing even when they look and sound a bit cheesy.

St John's Eve is more my thing.

St John's Eve derives from the time when Christian folk religion sought to accommodate older pagan practices. This traditional British midsummer festival is celebrated on 23rd June. In Celtic Britain and Ireland it was a time for bonfires. The farmers would jump over them, or drive their cattle between two fires – a symbolic blessing and a literal act of purification, fumigation. There'd be music and mischief and merry-making, with young lovers slipping away for illicit liaisons in the cornfields – and, doubtless, new lives conceived.

It's the night before the feast day of St John the Baptist, the voice in the wilderness, the desert prophet who baptised Jesus in the River Jordan. When Salome danced for Herod, for her reward she claimed John's decapitated head. As the early Church assimilated pre-Christian solar festivals, it placed St John at midsummer and Christ at the contrary Winter Solstice. In The Gospel of John, The Baptist tells us:

I am not the Christ, but that I am sent before him... He must increase, but I must decrease.

The image of Christ supplanting John subtly connects them with the solar cycle – the sun decreasing from midsummer, to rekindle at the Winter Solstice.

I've recently been reading *The High History of the Holy Grail* in which one of the many holy relics to be won is the sword that beheaded John the Baptist. When drawn from its scabbard it is still wet with blood.

23rd June is the night of the 205th consecutive monthly Cross Bones Vigil. To honour it, and St John's Eve, Katy and I invite five friends who have a loose connection with the south London graveyard to celebrate with us in our Glastonbury garden.

It's a beautiful evening with a single hieroglyphic wisp of cirrus cloud high in the sky, a winged spine stretched out in the blue.

We follow the ritual forms, freely adapting to happen-stance. I'm about to open the ceremony with seven chimes when the bell of St John the Baptist, whose tower we see from the garden, strikes the hour.

In the Bardic Offerings, James talks about John the Baptist, the Water Man, and how water is the agent of rebirth and psychic transformation. And of the resonance between John and Orpheus, both poets and prophets, water men, decapitated by women, their heads taking on a kind of immortality, the talking heads of a living myth.

I'm listening entranced, and think of the head of Bran the Blessed, the legend recorded in the second branch of the *Mabinogi*. Bran is Old Welsh for 'Crow', and the story has always resonated with me. Fatally wounded during the doomed Welsh raid on Ireland, Bran asks his companions to cut off his head. The head continues to speak, consoling, inspiring and generally entertaining Taliesin and the rest of the seven survivors. They eventually bury the head, on Bran's orders, on the White Hill guarding the Thames estuary at the gateway to London, to protect these islands from invasion.

Annabel does her own dark/light and lovely poem. Steve sings *The Water Song* by the Incredible String Band. Sally tells of an old relative in Ireland who could remember when they used to drive the cattle between the rows of fire, how the fiddlers and dancers would at carouse at the cross-roads until the priest came to remind them they were doing the Devil's Work. Everyone would stop, suitably shamefaced and repentant, to strike up as soon as the Father was gone.

I sing my song for St John's Eve, *Spark In The Dark*, a song of the love between the Earth and Sky, their separation and ultimate reunion. Many cultures conceive of a Sky God and Earth Goddess but these gendered roles are by no means absolute. The ancient Egyptians envisioned the cosmic pairing as Geb, the Earth God, and Nut, the Sky Goddess who gives birth not only to life on Earth but to all orders of being in the Universe.

Spark In The Dark

Hark! Hark! A Spark in the Dark
In the Dance of Death and Rebirth,
The Son of the Sky look down from on high
In Love with The Daughter of the Earth.

Son steal a horse from his Father's house.
Seven long nights he ride.
Until he come to the Earth Woman tent
And she open and she led him inside.

Hark! Hark! A Spark in the Dark
In the Dance of Death and Rebirth,
The Son of the Sky is come down from on high
In Love with The Daughter of the Earth.

Then the Men of the Law come a knockin' at the door
And they say that The Son must die,
To atone for the shame to his Father's Name,
And they hang him on a tree to dry.

Hark! Hark! A Spark in the Dark
In the Dance of Death and Rebirth,
The Son of the Sky is condemned to die
For Love of The Daughter of the Earth.

Daughter take the broken Son
And she put him back together.
And she give him kiss of life.
Now they live forever

In the Spirit, in the Flesh,
In the Fire, in the Water,
Where the Sky and Earth mesh
In The Son, in The Daughter.

Hark! Hark! A Spark in the Dark
In the Dance of Death and Rebirth,
The Son of the Sky is arisen on high
With the beautiful Bride of the Earth.

The Call

St John’s Eve and we’re
down the King Arthur, fired-up
for the new adventure.

First night out of lockdown
and the long winter waste with Arthur
worming in and out of K-holes.

Now The Word is
Arthur is clean and all set
to get Questing...

when...

Three leery Damsels
troll in, puffing
their fluff, one wielding

a chopped-off head,
sprayed gold –
some say lead –

anyway, now well
and truly
dead, shutting

the pub din
            to a pin
drop.

‘Namaste, Goddesses’
says Arthur, cucumber cool.
‘What’s with the bonce?’

Damsel with the head spells it out:
why The King and The Land
be laid to waste, branch and root,

and all because
some silly boy
neglected to say the magic word.

Hence the bonce and plenty more
where that came from
in the truck out front

and how come
she herself be
bald as a Buddhist coot.

And how now there’s nowhere left to hide.
This is The Call to all Good Knights
to ride. Ride! Ride!

The lads look shifty, eyeing up Damsel
Number Three in the short skirt
with the whip. ‘She’s well fit!’

‘I’d do ‘er up against the wall.’

Even so, Goddesses
Witches or just plain
lippy Avalon Damsels,

when one of ‘em’s packing
some poor Knight’s chopped-off and now
well and truly Dead

Head,

you don’t argue.

You don’t refuse The Call.

The Hole In The Ground

Glastonbury Festival
alternative 50th anniversary tribute

2020 marked the *official* 50th anniversary of the Glastonbury Festival. Back in the summer of 1970 the 'Pilton Pop, Folk and Blues festival' had attracted a thousand festival pioneers to Worthy Farm, each paying £1 to hear Tyrannosaurus Rex and a scratch line-up play in one of Farmer Eavis' fallow fields. Around that time, I was a teenage boy from the sticks, fresh out of school. Some friends and I had rented a cottage in the Welsh hills, where we'd recently blown our minds on some very strong acid – one night I'd shape-shifted into a crow! We were eager to connect with the flowering subculture, which we knew mainly from TV and magazine reports, but weren't sure where to find it. We weren't even aware of the Pilton gathering.

2021 was *our* 50th anniversary year. For us, and 12,000 free spirits, and for The Pyramid Stage itself, the *first* Glastonbury Festival happened on and around the 1971 summer solstice. And it was Free.

By then, I was a fully fledged Freak ('Don't call me Hippie!') 18 ¾, on the brink of dropping out of Cambridge to grow organic carrots on a Welsh commune. We'd heard rumours of a Free Festival in Glastonbury: that the costs were being covered by a few wealthy heads, including Winston Churchill's granddaughter Arabella, and that Somerset farmer Michael Eavis was somehow behind it and providing the fields. Where we came from, farmers were pragmatic, unsentimental types; they used to shoot crows and hang them in trees to scare the others. So Eavis quickly acquired a semi-mythical status.

We hitched down to Glastonbury, then a conservative Somerset market-town. With our long-hair, bare feet and cheesecloth robes, we must have looked like Biblical extras (though we considered ourselves Pantheists); we got lots of disapproving looks and some outright hostility. So it was a relief coming into the fields to see all the Freaks, the ones who looked like us, or at least like the people we aspired to be: 'the people our parents warned us against'.

We hadn't even brought a tent; we constructed a rudimentary bender by a hedge. My friends from Uni showed up better prepared, pitching their tents to form a semi-circle around our campfire. From here we could survey the whole festival site, looking down a gentle slope towards the Pyramid Stage. Music drifted up from the stage, and from acoustic jams and impromptu bands with battery-powered amps that struck up all around the fields, creating little hot spots of pleasure within the collective Body.

Ah, the Body! In 1971, England (not to mention Wales!) was a sexually uptight place. This was the first time I'd seen beautiful women and men, naked, unashamed, glorying in their nakedness. It was the first time I'd got naked in public. It was all deliciously sensual and innocent, with many a frolic in the long grass, but no coercion, no furtive groping. Everyone openly admiring and delighting in delighting one another: group hugs and body-painting, singalongs and spontaneous dance circles.

There was a real sense of anything goes, balanced by a sensitivity to others. Just the feel of the place was empowering and encouraged everyone to make it work. When I was coming down from an acid trip I found myself in the Release tent. Asked if I could help. Minutes later I found myself in the bad trips tent with a frightened young man, just being with him until he came down and started to see the funny side. It's maybe the first time I gave shamanic healing, without the self-consciousness that comes when you call it that.

Even the food was free: 'donations welcome'. Every evening The Diggers drove round the site in a land-rover and we threw money in the back to buy the next day's free food for all. And it was quality: organic, vegetarian meals; huge vats of curry and rice with all the trimmings; the breakfast table heaped with muesli, granola, fruit, nuts, yogurt – all this back in the day when even such foods were considered outlandish, foreign, borderline subversive.

And the stage: the first *ever* Pyramid Stage. It was the biggest pyramid I'd seen and when it lit up at night it felt like an initiation into the Earth Mysteries complete with visions of Ancient Egypt. And it wasn't all about the bands; all kinds of activists and seekers and dodgy geezers got up there for their moment on the mic. Guru Maharaj Ji flew in by helicopter to tell us there was no reason why God shouldn't fly in by helicopter. We were more impressed by the old American vegetarian freak with the pet chicken perched on his shoulder.

People took the mic to warn of 'bad acid' (rumour unconfirmed) or to promote their own 'amazing acid'. Someone put it out that two vendors wanted to sell hot-dogs on site. 'Yes, they can, so long as they drop acid.' Which they promptly did, and spent the night giving away free hot-dogs to anyone who'd eat them!

And yes, some fine music – Traffic, Family, Hawkwind, Quintessence, Gong, Melanie. And David Bowie – then a relatively minor star, though me and the North Wales contingent were fans. On the afternoon of 22nd June, we took an acid trip, timing our drop so as to peak during Bowie's set in the evening. Everything over-ran and he finally came on around dawn on the 23rd. I was in my sleeping bag in front of the Pyramid Stage, tuning in to snatches of songs and dimly aware that Bowie was on-stage just above me. As the sun came up, he sang *Memory of a Free Festival*. I crawled out of my sleeping bag, bleary-eyed and frog-throated, in time to sing along: 'The sun machine is coming down and we're gonna have a party'.

During the acid trip, we'd observed that there appeared to be two suns in the sky. We were discussing group hallucinations when the man on the mic said: 'See that UFO flying up by the sun?' Then, addressing the mysterious orb, he said: 'I don't know who or what you are, Man, but this is for you.' And the sound-system played Hendrix, *Third Stone From The Sun*.

After the festival, we returned to our Welsh cottage. The carrot crop failed. I went back to Cambridge, mostly to please my Dad. I reckoned I'd given him enough grief with drugs, politics, mysticism and free love. I read English, but spent most of my time studying magic and came out with a Third Class Degree. I don't regret a single step on the crooked way that led me to where I am now. I'd come away from that first Glastonbury Festival a changed boy-man. My collectivist ideals, my interest in esoteric wisdom and live performance, my entire life was shaped by it.

It was nearly thirty years before I went back. I reckoned that 1971 initiation was as good as it gets and didn't want to spoil the memory. In those intervening years, I travelled and studied widely, getting some grounding in shamanistic techniques, learning to integrate those youthful acid visions and to navigate between worlds. I lived a charmed life, earning a modest living as a writer and performer, operating at the interface of theatre and magic.

In the last days of 1999, I was being John Crow, performing my shamanic raps and street-rituals in the fortnightly 24-hour *Warp* parties ('Glastonbury without the mud') staged in The Drome (the railway arches under London Bridge Station – now a shopping-mall in the dead footprint of The Shard). There I got to know Pok and The Space Goats, who got me a gig in the Green Futures field at Glastonbury.

By then, the year 2000, the Festival was something else entirely, with 100,000 paying punters and maybe another 150,000 coming in over the fence: old freaks and travellers, punks and party people, city-slickers and ketamine/cider warriors. It still had its Pyramid stage - at the centre of a matrix of giant stages, each pumping out its own music in a Babylon of freak-shows and sprawling campsites, Gardens of Earthly Delight, portaloo parks and muddy mosh-pits. And, up in the Green Fields, you could catch the feel of that original Free Festival.

Katy Kaos and I came back every year thereafter with a small crew to do our Goose and Crow thing in the Green Futures field, on the Small World and Tadpole stages. In the Mandala Tent we hosted 'The Palace of Wisdom', an all-night Blakean Bardic poetry happening. Around 3am this scary northern punk took the stage; said he wasn't a poet but we should know about his music. At the end of his inspired rant, I said: 'You're a poet, you just don't know it.' And he said 'You're in my band'. Turned out he was Ron Tree, former Hawkwind bass-player. Next night, he got me up on the Avalon Stage to rap with Nik Turner's band.

Glastonbury is about creative sharing and serendipity, the random, magic moments: reconnecting with old mates and making new ones, sharing songs and stories round a campfire at dawn. Over the next twenty years we also chanced on some unforgettable live sets, from headline legends to bands we'd never heard of. We somehow contrived to miss Bowie's triumphant return, and even missed Stevie Wonder – we were off in the Green Fields chillin' to Reggae and Dub on the Rinky Dink sound system!

One night, Katy and I wandered up into the Craft Field and literally fell into The Hole In the Ground – soon to become legendary as the Underground Piano Bar – a subterranean amphitheatre dug into the hillside, operated by a fearsome Irish crew. We felt like we'd fallen into *Tír na nÓg*. I became part of their in-house cast of musicians, poets, burlesque artists and all-round hell-raisers.

We got thrown out of the Craft Field (for operating an illegal bar) and moved up above The Stones into the woods near the perimeter fence. The crew delighted in making The Hole hard to find; it was all word of mouth, a best-kept secret (until Eavis outed it as his pick of the Festival). We were sworn to deny any knowledge of its existence, on the occult principle that: 'If you're meant to be here, you'll find a way!' So many wild visionary nights fuelled by Paddy Bloomer's 'deadly' *poitín!*

In September 2020, Katy and I moved to Glastonbury, the town, completing a pilgrimage that for me had begun fifty years before. The Festival was postponed due to the restrictions that had impacted all our lives and decimated Music and the Arts. It was much missed.

I wrote to Michael Eavis, offering him a free private performance in the overgrown amphitheatre, the old Hole In The Ground. He didn't take up the offer or answer personally, but one of his team, the friendly and helpful Aoife, gave permission for our site visit. We drove to the Mary Gate and walked down the now-dry 'Muddy Lane'. Without the festival, the fields were at first unrecognisable, but every step heightened the sense of familiarity and deja-vu. Through the grove of trees, we glimpsed an imposing children's play castle with towers and turrets, painted pink, a vision of Camelot straight out of the Grail Legends.

The skeleton of the Pyramid Stage was still standing in an otherwise empty field. Taking our orientation from there, we soon made our way up to The Green Fields. At the bridge we remembered the food stall run by a West Midlands Indian family, where we often ate on our first night at the Festival. From there on, we could re-imagine all the old landmarks, projecting them onto the blank canvas of green meadows – the Greenpeace Field, the big toilet block at the crossroads, Croissant Neuf and Groovy Movie, the bandstand and the lake, the Crafts Field, Green Futures, The Healing Field – on so on up to The Stones, over the little bridge to the Dragon Field, our campsite and Festie Central for the best part of a decade, then up the hill to the overgrown shell of my favourite performance space. Aoife had sent an email politely asking us not to go inside the now derelict Piano Bar, warning us that the structure was very unstable. Fortunately it arrived after we'd set off, so we didn't consciously disobey her.

The stage was still standing, though the floor felt paper thin and I stepped gingerly. Accompanying myself on the bodhran, I sang *The Once In A Blue Moon Shebeen*, the fairy song which this place in an earlier incarnation had once inspired in me. I sang it to Katy, and to all incarnate and discarnate spirits who might be listening. Katy sat in the otherwise empty amphitheatre, the pit with its circle of steps cut in the earth and its crudely-hewn timber benches. The cockpit of Jon Brimble and Paddy's old bar was still intact, with the tiny stage on its roof where I once scared the hell out of a last-night crowd with a *John Crow Trickster* intervention. Now, in its dereliction, the skeletal timbers silhouetted against the sunset, the entire place felt haunted by the spirits of those nights gone by.

This return to Worthy Farm and The Hole In The Ground was itself a kind of pilgrimage – to what for us is forever a sacred site, where we've survived many a life-changing initiation. It was 23rd April, St George' Day, an important date in the Cross Bones calendar, and the evening of the 203rd consecutive monthly Vigil at the Cross Bones shrine. We came here on a mission, with a clear intention: to amplify the Glastonbury-Crossbones current.

We conducted a simple ceremony, tuning in on the Astral with our friends conducting the Vigil at the Cross Bones Graveyard Shrine, linking up on Zoom, or connecting from around the world.

On the stroke of seven, we rang the chimes and welcomed the spirits of the dead and the living. We held a candle to light the pathways, then laid Katy's flower petals on our improvised shrine. For the Bardic offering I recited *I Am The Wind* from *The Southwark Mysteries*. As ever in the Vigils, we closed the ritual with a circle of gin, repeating 'Life, Health, Happiness, Open Pathways' and the Unconditional Goose Blessing.

And we saw two suns! We were walking back through the fields as the sun was setting, when we observed what may have been light reflected on the clouds. It looked like a smaller, second sun, tinged with rainbow hues. With Goose and Crow Magic, you take your affirmations where you find them. We took this and drove home, feeling well affirmed.

We return on the evening of Friday 25th June 2021, past the Pyramid Field, through The Green Fields, to revisit the Hole In The Ground, now overgrown with nettles and thistles.

This time we leave the ruined stage in peace. We don't need to do another ritual; we've done our Cross Bones Vigil on St John's Eve, just two days ago. We picnic on the site of our caravan in the Dragon Field, which two years ago the amazing Irish crew had contrived to tow on site for us. The grass is long and green and buttercup yellow.

Exactly two years before it would have been kicking on the main stages, and we'd have been firing up to open the Underground Piano Bar at midnight. Now we look down across what was once the throbbing Heart of Babylon, recalling unforgettable sets – Radiohead, Leftfield, Faithless, Arthur Lee – hallucinatory nights in the Theatre and Circus Fields, lost weekends in Lost Vagueness, and a myriad magic moments each connected with a particular field.

The ghosts and echoes and flashbacks from our last twenty years of Glastonbury Festivals imprinted in SpaceTime grids, superimposed on verdant meadows now silent but for the strands of evening birdsong.

I look over to the hills on the far side, where the 18 ¾ year old me once erected a rickety bender. That was the first time I ever saw this landscape, and suddenly, for the first time in fifty years, I see it again as I saw it then.

In Eternity.

The Once In A Blue Moon Shebeen

In a hole in the ground on the wrong side of town,
Where you go to get lost so you can get found.
She wore a pink silk dress and her hair was a mess.
She was putting it about. She was putting it round.

And when she smiled you could see the wild child,
Though her eyes old and wise with the things that
she'd seen.
And you fall in love with Marie La Gauche
In The Once In A Blue Moon Shebeen.

Moonlight Serenade as the house-lights did fade
And she sang of the World before it was made,
Of the Daughters of Light and their crossing by night,
Of the deal that was done and the price that was paid.

Now she's working the crowd. She's laughing too loud.
Her lipstick is smeared and she tastes of poitín.
And you fall in love with Marie La Gauche
In The Once In A Blue Moon Shebeen.

O I laughed, I cried, I thought I had died,
As the band played a reel fit to heal The Divide.
When they hit the lost chords there was blood on the
boards,
And I swore by that blood she'd be my Fairy Bride.

And she said: Hold me tight, we have only the night.
In the cold light of day this'll fade like a dream…

I woke in a field with the dew on my face.
The Blue Moon Shebeen was gone without trace.
There was no going back, so I had to go on.
Though I wander the Earth I still walk in her grace.

In a shoe-box altar, in a travellers' shelter,
In the wind and the rain, in the wild and the green,
I fell in love with Marie La Gauche
In The Once In A Blue Moon Shebeen.

Mary Magdalene

Down a passage off Magdalene Street is a former hospice for pilgrims visiting The Abbey. The Pilgrims' Hospital was founded in 1250 AD. In the 15th century the hall of the hospice was replaced by the Magdalene Almshouses for the ageing poor of the parish. Five of the eleven almshouses remain, now adjoining a strip of walled garden. The simple, bare chapel is dedicated to St Margaret of Scotland but is often referred to as the Magdalene Chapel.

Mary Magdalene was surely in the thoughts and prayers of many a pilgrim who came here in hope of curing physical or spiritual wounds. It's a place where we too can meditate on her story, her agency to heal and to transform, and how she can teach us to grow not in spite of but precisely because of our human imperfections.

In the *Gospel of St John* she is the woman who meets and speaks with the risen Christ in the garden. She brings the news of his resurrection to the male Apostles, who at first refuse to believe her. They know only that the grave was empty. To them Christ is an absence. To Mary he is a presence so tangible that he had to ask her not to touch him 'because I am not yet ascended'. He spoke to her tenderly and gave her comfort.

The early Church fathers recognised her as the 'Apostle of the Apostles', but by the end of the 6th century the Church had begun to reinvent her as the 'penitent sinner'. The revised image conflated several women mentioned in the canonical gospels.

Mary Magdalene is named as the woman from whom Jesus drives out seven devils. Medieval church commentators saw these devils as representing the Seven Deadly Sins. Revisiting the scene with more empathetic eyes, we see Jesus laying on hands to calm and heal an epileptic fit, a bi-polar crisis or a psychotic episode. Or perhaps this simply refers to an act of initiation. For this is the woman who will become his chosen disciple.

There's also Mary of Bethany, who washed Jesus' feet and listened to his teachings while her sister Martha complained about having to do all the cooking. Jesus later raised her brother Lazarus from the dead, though not before Mary had given him a piece of her mind for not coming in time to save him.

Then there's the woman who 'was taken in adultery, in the very act'. She's brought before Jesus by the Scribes and Pharisees so as to test this upstart Teacher of the New Law. The law of Moses commands 'that such should be stoned' - but Jesus intervenes to save her:

He that is without sin among you, let him cast the first stone at her. [1]

Not forgetting the unnamed sinner in the house of Simon the Pharisee, who anointed him and dried his feet with her hair:

Her sins, which are many, are forgiven; for she loved much. [2]

In 591 AD Pope Gregory I ruled that all the above-mentioned women were one and the same. Just as the Church had emphasised the immaculate virginity of Mary the Mother of God, so this other Mary, this Magdalene, became the repository for the patriarchal Church's conflicted desire and disgust when faced with female sexuality.

Yet even this fabricated Mary Magdalene seems to have taken on the power to inspire and comfort, to heal and change lives, especially the lives are those living on the edge. In medieval times the cult of The Magdalene established itself in folk-religion, tempering the harsh laws of the patriarchy.

The cult especially attracted women. It allowed them a place to express their own agency, their yearning for Divine Consummation. Devotees would fast and pray to enter ecstatic trances, or weep for days and nights, lamenting the physical suffering of Our Lord, consciously channelling Mary Magdalene and Her intimate relations with Jesus Himself. 'Maudlin', a medieval variant of Magdalene or Maudelyn, came to mean 'tearful' and is often associated with sentimental drunks. But then The Magdalene would surely include alcoholics – and drug addicts too – in her street Church of the Outcast.

In 1945, the rediscovery of the *Nag Hammadi* scrolls and other lost Gnostic manuscripts radically expanded our understanding of early Christianity. They recorded the esoteric teachings of mystery schools and desert communities from the 2nd and 3rd centuries AD.

The Gnostics practised a discipline designed to liberate the spark of Divinity trapped in matter. Far from being the Son of the Creator God, their Christ comes to set us free from the ignorance in which we objectify and then unthinkingly worship our Creator.

One of their most idiosyncratic texts, the *Pistis Sophia,* was rediscovered in 1773. It charts the fall of Sophia, the 'thirteenth aeon', into the material universe, and her ultimate restoration to her true place. The text is presented as the Resurrected Jesus teaching his disciples, initiating them into his esoteric teachings. Mary Magdalene takes the lead in questioning him and he praises her for helping him to elucidate the Mystery.

In one of the *Nag Hammadi* texts, the *Dialogue of the Saviour,* Christ recognises that Mary Magdalene has a special part to play in the Unfolding:

You make clear the abundance of the revealer.[3]

In *The Gospel of Philip* she is called 'the Consort of the Saviour' and Christ promises that she will be united with him 'in the Bridal Chamber'. Philip also tells us that Christ:

loved her more than the other disciples and would kiss her on the mouth. They said to him, 'Why do you love her more than us?'[4]

In her own *Gospel of Mary,* Mary Magdalene reveals to the disciples the secret teachings that Christ transmitted to her personally. In this, as in several other texts, Peter is troubled by her special relationship with the Saviour:

'Did he really speak with a woman without our knowledge (and) not openly? Are we to turn about and all listen to her? Did he prefer her to us?'[5]

The heretical notion that Jesus and Mary Magdalene married and had children has been in circulation for centuries, despite the best efforts of the Church to suppress it. The story was current in the 1970s; the psychedelic rock band Jefferson Airplane spelled it out in their song *The Son of Jesus*. In 1982 the publication of *Holy Blood, Holy Grail* introduced the story to a wider audience. The authors reinterpreted the legend of the Holy Grail as Mary Magdalene's womb and the royal blood-line descended from her and Jesus. In their reading 'Saint Graal' (Holy Grail) revealed its hidden meaning as 'Sang Real' (Blood Royal). It formed the basis for Dan Brown's 2003 novel *The Da Vinci Code*. Such ideas were ridiculed by academic historians and theologians, but took hold in the popular imagination.

Unsurprisingly, Glastonbury has derived its own version of the legend, in which Jesus, Mary Magdalene and their child visit the town. Evidence for this is even more elusive than the records of Joseph of Arimathea's visit. As a poetic truth, it is powerful and evocative. In our magical works, let us create a safe space to receive Jesus, The Magdalene and The Child.

In *The Southwark Mysteries*, The Goose reiterates her heresy:

That the Magdalene Whore
A love child bore
To the dancing Lord of The Liberty.[6]

She self-identifies with sex workers and outcasts, with a spiritual work that is practised not in church but at street shrines and in unconsecrated graveyards.

Through a process of Chinese whispers, the late Dean of Southwark Cathedral, The Very Revd. Colin Slee, heard that I was writing a 'Southwark Mystery Play'. At the time, *The Southwark Mysteries* existed only as the verses received from The Goose. I hadn't planned to write a Mystery Play. But Colin encouraged me, and The Goose gave many signs and affirmations, so I took it on. As the work evolved, our meetings became like theological wrestling matches, as Colin strove to impress on me 'what you need in a Mystery Play'. He expressed concern at my play's pagan elements and especially at 'the references to God as female', while I staunchly defended my vision of The Goose as a manifestation of Mary Magdalene. It was The Magdalene who helped us find common ground.

The Mystery Play was performed on 23rd April 2000 in Shakespeare's Globe and Southwark Cathedral. In it The Goose acts out aspects of the Church's composite Magdalene. She's possessed by Seven Devils (represented as tabloid paparazzi) which Jesus expels. Later she anoints him – and is defended by him when Judas accuses her of wasting the precious oil.

In writing *The Southwark Mysteries* I came to see the question as to whether Jesus and Mary had children as a distraction. 'The Child' is the esoteric doctrines he passed down to her, transmitted not in Holy Books but in songs, plays and stories, in theatres, taverns and brothels. Near the end Jesus tells Peter:

Peter, of my Church, I made you the Head,
But it takes a Magdalene to open its Heart.[7]

From medieval times The Abbey's west wall was bounded, appropriately enough, by Magdalene Street. Across the road Cock Lane ran down by St Benignus Church into Grope Cunt Lane. The name was used in many English cities as a no-nonsense description of what went on in what we now more discreetly call 'Red Light Districts'. There was a Grope Cunt Lane in London, referred to in *The Southwark Mysteries.* Our Glastonbury 'Lane' is a short hop from The Abbey; it's easy to imagine the monks being led astray there.

A relatively recent mural in St Patrick's Chapel revives the medieval image of Mary Magdalene as the emblematic sinner, possessed by Seven Devils or Deadly Sins. The 'Sins' are depicted as little cartoons – gluttony, lust and so on – being spat out by dragons. These dragons are bound to her body – or perhaps erupting from it, prefiguring that scene in *Alien*. The seventh devil is still within her, the Sin of Pride.

The first time I saw it, I was disturbed by the way it objectified Mary Magdalene, completely obscuring the qualities of love, self-healing and awakened consciousness that Jesus so clearly recognised in her. Deliberately or unconsciously, it reiterates those old patriarchal projections, like an evil spell cast to bind the Magdalene and Her agency.

One morning in the Chapel, I cast a spell to reclaim Our Magdalene, to free Her from the judgement of men. There are lots of us casting spells in Glastonbury. Sometimes the spells cancel each other out! A good rule of thumb: if your spell is true, it will ring true and so manifest itself. Why waste psychic energy trying to impose our spells on others?

Working with The Magdalene can bring up our own loss, pain and trauma. This can lead to an identification with the Magdalene persona, and to acting out – often to the irritation of others who may see it as attention-seeking behaviour! Let's be compassionate: if people act out, maybe they're trying to attract God's attention, to get some higher power to notice their personal predicament. If you see yourself doing it, just observe dispassionately. Breathe. See it for what it is – a catharsis, part of the healing process, not a state to get stuck in.

When conducting psychic healing work with The Magdalene, as with The Goose, I've found it helpful to cultivate the state of shining emptiness, to create a safe space in which to receive Her.

You may find Her in a peaceful place of contemplation, in her Chapel and Almshouses, in The Roman Catholic Church of Our Lady St Mary of Glastonbury, or in the Goddess Temple – all on a short stretch of Magdalene Street. You might equally find Her with the Hare Krishnas serving free food outside St John's Church, or in the travellers' camp at Beckery, close to the site of Her Chapel on Bridie's Mound. When we can see Her at work in others, especially those who live more on the edge than we do, only then do we truly begin to comprehend Her.

Of course you don't have to be in Glastonbury to commune with Mary Magdalene, or any other spiritual agency. I served Her as The Goose for 23 years at Cross Bones, then I walked Her out into the world, to honour Her at sacred sites around these islands. I found She loved the wild places and the liminal, contested areas of sacred ground, not official heritage sites but places on the edge that cry out for healing and consecration, places where Leonard Cohen's 'crack in everything' let's 'the light get in'.

As a channel of the Magdalene Current, The Goose is primarily an agency of healing and reconciliation. She is invoked to turn us away from judgement to compassion for others – and, no less crucially, for ourselves.

The healing of rifts and divisions is manifested on many levels. Conceived as The Divine Feminine incarnate in a sex worker, The Goose-Magdalene is vitally engaged in the work of sexual healing. In this aspect, she can be evoked in each of us personally, to heal our most intimate sexual and emotional wounds.

In our collective spiritual experience, she mediates to reconcile the tensions between the spirit and the flesh, which were amplified by the teachings of the Christian Church going back to St Augustine.

The Goose-Magdalene goes far beyond consecrating the pleasures of the senses. On the deepest levels She's here to heal the rifts between 'mind' and 'matter', to reveal 'The Spirit in the flesh, the Sacred in the profane, Eternity in time.'

[1] *The Gospel of John* 8
[2] *The Gospel of Luke* 7
[3] *The Dialogue of the Saviour* (trans. Emmel, Koester, Pagels) The *Nag Hammadi* Library *(NHL)* 1988
[4] *The Gospel of Philip*
[5] *The Gospel of Mary* (trans. King, MacRae, Wilson, Parrott) *NHL* 1988
[6] *The Southwark Mysteries,* John Constable 1996
[7] *The Southwark Mysteries*, Constable

The Ballad of Grope Cunt Lane

In Glastonbury Abbey, the monk reads his Bible
In a bare cloistered candle-lit hall.
His world is in order, his steps well-rehearsed
As he answers the Vespers call.

And there with the Brothers as he praises Our Lady
He ponders how Our Lord was scorned,
Scourged and nailed to a Cross
For Man's profit – God's loss!
The King with His Crown of Thorns.

And he fixes his thought
On how Man's Soul was bought
And paid for with God's Death and pain,
But then his mind starts to twitch.
He's getting the itch
To take a wander down Grope Cunt Lane.

It troubles his heart, as he paces the orchard
And over by the old fish-pond.
He knows he has pledged to resist Temptation
For the promise of The World Beyond.

Yet, he argues, if God didn't mean us to stray
He wouldn't have given us feet.
So, as darkness does fall,
He shins over the wall
And scuttles cross Magdalene Street.

And She's standing there
With a rose in her hair
And a halo of soft, summer rain.
Then She leads him in
To her Den of Sin
On the corner of Grope Cunt Lane.

In the meanest of slums, with a child in a cot
And a crucifix nailed to the wall,
He's thinking about the Garden of Eden,
St Augustine and his Fall.

But as She opens the buds of sensual desire,
He glimpses a World made whole,
Where God is revealed
When a Body is healed,
No less than when shriving a Soul.

And for one moment there
It's too much to bear
The thought that His God, once contained
Within Hallowed Grounds,
Is now doing His rounds
In a hovel down Grope Cunt Lane.

Dawn finds him, distracted, in Our Lady's Chapel
But now every prayer bears his taint.
He feels that with every step that he takes
He's defiling the bones of a saint.

At Matins, he goads himself to remember
How he once took a vow to be chaste.

But now Vespers is sung
The vow is undone
By the Apple and its after-taste.

So he dons his hair-shirt,
Eats maggots and dirt,
But his Demon still drives him insane,
For his Soul is at war,
Now he curses the Whore
Who led him down Grope Cunt Lane.

The kindly old Abbot reminds him
That it's only human to fall.
The monk throws forgiveness back in his face,
Denouncing the Sins of them all.

He storms out to preach in the Market Place
On the Flesh, the Devil and Lust,
How the birds of the air
And the flowers so fair
Must wither to ashes and dust.

He may wash his foul Soul
Hang it out on a pole
But he cannot get rid of the stain,
He cannot unknow
The Apples that grow
In that garden down Grope Cunt Lane.

Meanwhile, the Woman has more on her mind
Than saving her God-given Soul,
There's a rent to be paid and a child to be fed
And a dream to be out of this hole.

As, with coins likely filched from the Almoner's tin,
The monks form an orderly queue
For to step in the door,
For to dance with the Whore
Or to simmer a while in her Stew.

And such venial crimes
Scarce trouble their minds
Though for Lent they may sometimes abstain.
But our poor hapless monk
Is already punch-drunk
On the Knowledge of Grope Cunt Lane.

At The George and Pilgrim, he falls in with strangers,
They call themselves Friends of the King.
They ply him with flagons of Somerset cider,
Then he's fired up and ready to sing:

How the monks live in Vice and gross Luxury…
How they drain the life-blood of the poor…
The King's Friends go to town,
Tear the old Abbey down,
With the Abbot carved up on the Tor.

Then they plunder the stones
For the lead and the bones,
And, if any dare to complain,
Lay the blame on the monk
Who lay with the punk
In her hell-hole down Grope Cunt Lane.

In his madness, the monk tramps up Wearyall Hill,
Hangs himself from the old Holy Thorn.

But She cuts him down, cradles him in her arms,
Her voice cracked between pity and scorn...

‘Does it please your God if you blot out your life
And all that He made you to be?
Until you discover
Your God in The Other
From yourself you will never be free.

For though you aspire
To the Heavenly choir
You’ll be dragged down again and again,
Until you take a long look
At that God you mistook
For the Devil down Grope Cunt Lane.’

Good people of Glastonbury, prithee tell me
Which of these served God the best.
The woman, naked in more than Body?
Or the monk in his iron vest,

Who made of his Soul a theatre of pain,
Imprisoned his God in there?
Or a woman in need
Who did her best to feed
Her world with compassion and care?

The Mary whose Sin
Cannot even begin
To measure the Grace that sustains
Below, as above,
God’s undying Love
For His daughter down Grope Cunt Lane.

The Mural In St Patrick's Chapel

Glastonbury Abbey, for Raga

Incontinent priests! Pope Gregory sealed
their self-disgust to snag the painter's eye,

reduce Her to an emblem, a caution:
the rosy plump embodiment of Pride.

Mary Magdalene, with six of Her seven
devils extruded. Six dragons spew forth

pictographic Sins: the glutton
with fat pig; the lustful couple a-fuck.

I light a candle to cleanse and to reclaim
Our Mary, Priestess,

strip away their composite Whore-
cum-Crazy-Girl.

To conceive: six friendly dragons, to flap
and frolic in the lime-washed space.

Her Soul, at One
with Her Jesus and the Christ in Him.

Where's the seventh? That splotch
on her shoulder? Or still lodged

deep within? She whose Sin
is forgiven, for She loved much.

At Chalice Well

At Chalice Well
By the sign of the fish,

I wish.
I wish.

From Chalice Hill
I look up to The Tor.

With old Pilgrims' eyes
I see, as they saw.

22nd July. My 69th birthday. As a young thrill-seeker, I never seriously thought I'd live to be thirty – which then became forty, fifty, as I passed each landmark. Having been seriously ill in 2019, it's a wonder I'm here at all – let alone a Glastonbury resident!

Our friend Di the writer and theatre director is down from London to celebrate. Di and I were teenage lovers. We stormed through the '70s and '80s in an on-off relationship. By the '90s we'd settled on being good friends. Katy and Di have independently established a warm friendship.

The day before Katy had driven us to South Cadbury, a contender for the site of King Arthur's Camelot. As she'd hoped, Di loved the lush ferns and wild flowers of Castle Lane leading up Cadbury Hill, the overgrown fortifications, the view of the surrounding hills and meadows and the vast expanse of sky at the summit. We arranged to meet the following morning to celebrate my birthday at Chalice Well.

In pagan mythology, wells are sources of healing and shamanistic initiation, portals to the Otherworld. Their powers flowed seamlessly into Celtic Christianity. The 5th century Irish Saint Bride, Brid or Bridie, takes on the role of her pagan precursor Brigid, the protector of holy wells and springs. There's a Bride's Well at the foot of Bridie's Mound. Glastonbury and its environs has many wells, many of them long since blocked or overgrown. A trickle of water still splashes on the mossy stones at St Joseph's Well by his chapel in The

Abbey. The Mother of them all, still overflowing in its abundance, rises in the cleft between Chalice Hill and The Tor. Here two springs brim up in close proximity.

The crystal clear waters of the White Spring gush from a pipe on Well House Lane and feed the pools in the dark cavernous interior of a former waterworks building. Flickering candles and spontaneous bursts of chanting evoke the ambience of a temple. Naked devotees climb the steps to plunge in the healing waters.

The spring that feeds Chalice Well, which runs down channels through the terraced gardens, is stained rusty red with iron oxide, and is known as the Red or Blood Spring. Legend has it that Joseph of Arimathea buried or washed the chalice here, and that its waters run red with the blood of Christ.

We come across Di exercising, dangling from the branch of a yew tree in 'King Arthur's Court', where the waters of the Red Spring splash down red rocks into the Healing Pool and on through a stone channel to the Vesica Pool below.

On a hot summer's day, it's a relief to bathe our feet in the pool. Apart from its healing properties, the cool water is refreshing and energising. Katy tells a family from Wales about the virtues of the Red and White Springs, unselfconsciously speaking as the Voice of the Well.

We climb the winding paths up through the gardens, splashing our faces and drinking a few drops of the Blood Spring from the Lion's Head, then sit awhile by the Chalice Well. The Well Head is formed by a massive block of stone. Dion Fortune believed that a chamber opening out of the well-shaft was once used for human sacrifice, to appease 'the Old Gods and their dark powers':

This was no fountain hallowed by miracle and vision, but an ancient Druid place of sacrifice…

The Well is now a tranquil place for meditation and reconnection. Its wrought ironwork cover was designed and gifted in 1919 by Frederick Bligh Bond to Alice Buckton, she of the pageant film and then owner of the Chalice Well. The image is of a *vesica piscis* pierced by a lance, representing the union of contraries – male and female, Spirit and Nature, the inner and outer worlds. The image can also be seen on the wrought iron gates of the White Spring chamber.

We walk on up to the little alcove with a stone statue of Our Lady, where some have left candles, and explore the meadow at the top of the hill, together or apart for moments of solitude. We maintain silence until we've returned to where the water eddies and spirals down through iron-red stone chalices on its descent to the vesica pool. I admit to Di that I was a bit distracted by the attention-seeking behaviour of the 'Goddesses' at the Well who seemed to be 'acting out' their mystical experiences, self-consciously making magical passes.

Di is more generous, maybe more in tune with the healing energies: 'I just saw them dancing.'

Being born on 22nd July, the feast day of St Mary Magdalene, I was fated to be in her crew. Since the Cross Bones Vigils are held on the 23rd of every month, the 23rd July Vigil became our Isis-Magdalene Festival when I traditionally recited the Magdalene poems from

The Southwark Mysteries cycle. And so I did this year, holding a simple Glastonbury Vigil with Katy and Annabel in the churchyard of St Benignus.

I heard about The Festival of the Rose from Joseph the photographer and incense maker. I was instinctively drawn to this celebration of the mystical Way of The Rose 'in which the word of God made itself flesh'. The resonances of The Rose with Sufism, Mary Magdalene, Isis and other expressions of the Divine Feminine, are explored in books by Halima, the festival founder. Joseph put us in touch, but the performance slots were already booked.

As the festival opened, I ran into Joseph in the street. He invited me to perform a poem to open his Sacred Incense Workshop in the Magdalene Chapel. Standing behind an altar festooned with roses, I performed fragments from *The Southwark Mysteries* that channel and elevate The Magdalene. It was my first indoor performance in well over a year, and I was gratified that it was so well received by the sixteen people who filled the small chapel.

To get to honour Mary Magdalene in Her own chapel is a blessing in itself. Strictly speaking it's dedicated to St Margaret of Scotland. It adjoins the Magdalene Almshouses and devotees of Mary have rededicated it to Her. A few paces north on Magdalene Street stands the Roman Catholic church of Our Lady St Mary of Glastonbury with its statue of The Madonna and Child.

The following invocation is to Our Lady, The Mother of God known and worshipped under many names. In the Amazon, in the syncretic Santo Daime church, she is honoured as *Rainha da Floresta* (Queen of the Forest) and *Rainha da Lua* (Queen of the Moon).

Queen Of The Moon

Queen of the vision revealed in the vine
And the leaves of the shining tree,
Be here in our hearts. Let our hearts entwine.
Open our eyes to see.

Queen of the Moon and the blue green Earth
Crowned with the Stars and the Sun,
Be here in our dances of death and rebirth.
Here let your dance be done.

Queen of the voices that shine in the night
As we walk in the valley of fear,
Be here in our hearts. Fill our hearts with light.
Open our ears to hear.

Queen of the Moon and the blue green Earth
Crowned with the Stars and the Sun,
Be here in our dances of death and rebirth.
Here let your dance be done.

Brevis Vita Merlini[1]

Big Shot get the jitters
So he build himself a tower
To protect him from the meatheads
Come to muscle for his power.

Each day the tower rises
And every night it falls.
It’s as if some fairy power
Bewitched the tower walls.

So he go to see the wizards
And they say what’s to be done:
That the fairy curse can only be banished
By the blood of a fatherless son.

Out go the word and the word come back
With the lad with no Dad, and his Mum
Who swears he was not got with any mortal man
But by ‘some sexy Incubum’.

But the brat ain’t about to lay his sweet head
On some Sacrificial King-size chopping block.
‘Tell me,’ says he: ‘What be under the tower?
Under this very rock?

Dig down: you find a sweet-water lake.
Drain it: two eggs glow with light.
When they hatch, two Dragons fight in the sky.
Then the Red is struck down by the White.’

So they dig and they drain and it all come to pass
And just as the wild boy did warn.
Soon the old King is dead and a new King is come.
The boy prophet, Merlin, is born.

[1] Merlin's origin myth is told by Geoffrey of Monmouth in his *History of the Kings of Britain*. The old King is Vortigern. He had brought in Saxon mercenaries who quickly overran the land, forcing him to take refuge in his tower. Having solved the riddle of the falling tower, Merlin utters a stream of prophesies, commencing with the Saxon (White Dragon) subjugation of the Britons (The Red). He uses shape-shifting magic to effect the conception of the new King, Arthur, whose mentor he becomes.

The tower and the lake below it were in Wales at Dinas Emrys, named in Merlin's honour. In *The History of the Kings of Britain* Geoffrey drew on oral tradition, including the legend that Merlin magically transported the stones of The Giant's Dance from Ireland to Stonehenge.

Merlin is born of a mortal woman and an incubus. His death is equally ambivalent. In Welsh legend, he sleeps in a Glass Castle on Bardsey Island off the Llyn peninsula in North Wales – along with the thirteen treasures of Britain. In *The High History of The Holy Grail*, Arthur's Knights are shown Merlin's empty grave at Tintagel Castle and told how his body was 'snatched away, either on God's behalf or the Enemy's, but which we know not.'

Geoffrey's poem *Vita Merlini* presents an alternative life of Merlin. Seized by a prophetic madness, he becomes a wild man of the woods, questioning the very basis of existence. He comes to his senses by a healing fountain. This Merlin is initiated into star-lore and the mysteries of creation by Taliesin. He then renounces his occult powers and retires to a life of prayer and contemplation.

Once More For The Sexes

for Arthur and Guinevere

Man falls in love
with Woman and Her Mystery.
He'll not rest from His Quest
till he find Her True Word.

The Woman just wants
to be understood
and if not then at least
be heard.

The Quest for the Holy Grail is not a coherent, linear narrative. The versions written down in the 12th and 13th centuries are full of contradictions and contrasting outcomes. The most radical variant is entitled *Perlesvaus* (Perceval) or *Le Haut Livre de Saint Graal (The High History of The Holy Grail).*[1]

Professor Mary Williams remarks: '*Perlesvaus* differs in many respects from other versions, one of the most important being its close relation to Glastonbury Abbey.'[2] She suggests that it was expressly written to enhance The Abbey's prestige and to encourage support for its rebuilding after the devastating fire of 1184.

The High History of the Holy Grail introduces us to an Arthur very different from the heroic King of popular legend. He has become lazy and decadent; his reputation is fallen into disrepute; his court is idle and dissolute. In despair, Guinevere goads him to embark on a new adventure.

Arthur's Squire dreams he steals a golden candle-stick from a chapel as a gift for Arthur and is stabbed by its guardian. He wakes in a delirium, to find the knife still buried in him, and dies before dawn. A fatal wound received during Astral Travel!

Embarking on his new adventure, The King sees a hermit conducting the Mass in a Chapel. The entrance is psychically barred to him, but he glimpses a vision of Our Lady offering the Child to the hermit as the Sacrament. As he watches, the Child transmutes into the bleeding Christ, crowned with thorns, before changing back into 'the shape of the Child'.[3]

The Hermit chastises Arthur for having fallen from honour, and explains that the land is laid waste because of a Knight who stayed in the Castle of the Fisher King. When the Holy Grail appeared before him, he failed to ask the question: 'Whom does it serve?'

Arthur is wounded by The Black Knight, whom he slays. A Damsel tells him to cut off the Knight's Head, then uses the blood to wash and heal his wound. On his way home, Arthur hears a disembodied Voice urging him to hold court again. He returns triumphant, eager to share his adventures with Guinevere.

This first 'branch of The Holy Grail' acts not only as a dramatic prologue but also as a key to the esoteric meanings of the strange occurrences to come.

Many Knights answer Arthur's call to come to Court for the feast of St John, though Gawain and Lancelot are conspicuously absent. After the first serving, the feast is rudely interrupted by three enigmatic 'Damsels of the Car' bearing the decapitated heads of slain knights encased in gold, silver or lead. They deliver the shield that once belonged to Joseph of Arimathea, which is to be claimed by the Knight who shall ultimately 'achieve the Grail'.

They also bring news of The Fisher King and his 'languishment'. (This version of the legend makes no mention of the dolorous wound inflicted on him by the spear of Longinus.) They repeat that The Fisher King's travails and the blighted land are the fault of the Knight who, in the presence of the Holy Grail, neglected to ask: 'Whom does it serve?'

The story then takes up the separate adventures of Sir Gawain and Sir Lancelot as they independently pursue their dual quest: to journey to The Fisher King's Castle and to find the much heralded 'Best Knight' who is destined to find The Grail.

Gawain encounters a bewildering array of castles, each with its own peculiar enigma, of giants, dwarfs and knights to be fought and slain, and of Damsels in varying degrees of distress, whom he rescues or who do their best to seduce him. The narrative is repetitive, often inconsistent, bristling with grotesque imagery. When, despite Gawain's attempts to save him, King Gurgalain's son is killed by a giant, the King orders that his corpse be boiled, cut into small pieces and distributed among the nobles of the land.

Some of the Castles guard yet more Holy Relics. The Castle of the Golden Circlet holds Christ's Crown of Thorns, encased in gold. Perceval's sister Dindrane must go alone at night to the Graveyard Perilous to obtain a strip from the altar-cloth which had originally covered Christ in the Holy Sepulchre. This is to protect the knight who will defend her and her mother Yglais from a mortal enemy.

As a reward for fighting and killing the Giant who slew his son, King Gurgalain gifts Gawain the sword which cut off the head of St John the Baptist. When drawn from the scabbard it is wet with blood. Gawain eventually presents the sword to The Fisher King, to gain entry to the Castle of the Grail.

Throughout his quest, Gawain is repeatedly reminded that, if the Grail should appear to him, he must remember to ask the all-important question. This happens so often it becomes comic. In The Fisher King's Castle, Gawain witnesses no less than three appearances of The Grail. The other guests watch nervously, willing him to ask the question. Distracted by three drops of blood that fall from the tip of the bleeding lance, struck dumb between Grace and frailty, Gawain fails the test.

Lancelot fares no better. He too is received at the Grail Castle but, because of his illicit love for Queen Guinevere, he is denied even a fleeting vision of The Grail.

Perceval is regularly cited as the 'Best Knight' in the world, the only Knight worthy to receive The Grail. He alone can deliver his mother and sister from their enemies and restore the Seven Castles and the Vales they have lost. Yet if he seems cut out to be the Knight on the white charger, there are problematic aspects to his character. When still a lad, out of sympathy for a Knight under attack, or perhaps out of sheer youthful exuberance, he kills The Red Knight with his javelin, thereby provoking future acts of vengeance against his family.

Even when he finally comes to defeat his uncle, The Lord of the Moors, and so restore his mother Yglais' lands, she does not flinch from spelling out his shortcomings. She holds him to blame for The Fisher King's decline and recent death. Prior to his final battle, Yglais weighs the urge for retribution against the teaching of Solomon: 'how the sinner that curseth other sinner curseth himself likewise.'

Yet, having defeated The Lord of the Moors, Perceval enacts a brutal, bloody vengeance. He cuts off the heads of eleven Knights, filling a vat with their blood, in which the Lord of the Moors, bound hands and feet, is hung upside down until he's drowned.

For all this barbarism, Volume I of *Perlesvaus* ends with order restored to Arthur's realm. Early in Volume II two suns appear in the sky, their beams flooding the hall of Arthur's Court: a Voice tells the King it's a sign that Perceval has reclaimed the Castle of The Grail, telling him to go there on pilgrimage. All seems well, until another Damsel appears with a casket containing the decapitated head of Arthur's son Lohot, murdered by Kay the Seneschal. And then...

Things fall apart. Again. And again!

Jessie L. Weston finds the *Perlesvaus* version of the Grail story 'very unsatisfactory. The illness of the King is badly motivated, and he dies before the achievement of the Quest'.[4] It doesn't fit with her view of the Grail Romances as incomplete, degenerate remnants of ancient fertility rituals.

We shouldn't gloss over the inconsistencies or seek to excuse the darker aspects of the Grail legend and of the age that produced it. A world where gallant Knights rescue defenceless Damsels hardly stands up to feminist scrutiny – although, on closer inspection, it's usually the Damsels making the moves on the Knights, who struggle and squirm to defend their own chastity without causing offence!

Even leaving aside its gratuitous violence and casual anti-Semitism, there's a notable absence of Christian charity, mercy or forgiveness. On the surface the tale could be read as a crude manifesto for the Church Militant and for the crusading spirit of the Middle Ages. The Arthurian scholar Roger Loomis considered the author 'deranged', while Barbara Newman suggested that he may have been a veteran of the crusades suffering from post-traumatic stress disorder. The graphic decapitations and mutilations are all too familiar features of Holy Wars in the Middle East from the crusades to the present day.

Yet, if we approach *Perlesvaus* not as a literal but as a poetic truth, an esoteric initiation rite to be read symbolically, we will find much to inspire and inform our own spiritual journeys. Our hero has three distinct names – Perceval, Perlesvaus and Parluifet. In the tale itself, these first two names are interpreted as 'losing the vale, or vales', referring to the Seven Castles taken from his mother. Mary Williams offers an alternative, reading as 'passing through the vale, or vales', referring to the first and second degrees of an initiation rite. Perceval's third name, Par-lui-fet, means 'made of himself'. Professor Williams suggests that, to attain the third degree of the cult:

> *the candidate… must have become perfect (Parfet) through his own effort – Par-lui fet, only then can he penetrate the secret of the Grail.*[5]

As we follow Arthur, Gawain, Lancelot and Perceval himself on their individual adventures and frequent humiliations we see that each can only fulfil their individual potential. Each attains their own Degree of Initiation according to their capacity. They can only journey to where – and what – they truly are.

And what is it, this big question that everyone seems to know about yet forgets to ask?

The asking places the questioner in a dualistic relation to The Grail, as the recipient of its grace. It invites The Grail to answer by dissolving these boundaries, to reveal the underlying unity of all Being, the Divine Humanity questioning and answering itself, giving and receiving in a single, indivisible, transformational act.

Of course before we can put the question, we first have to find The Grail. But for when we do, it's as well to be prepared.

[1] *The High History of The Holy Grail* translated by Sebastian Evans (J.M. Dent & Co. 1898; The Lost Library, facsimile edition 2016)

[2] *Perlesvaus*, Mary Williams, published in *Glastonbury A Study In Patterns* (RILKO 1969)

[3] *The High History of The Holy Grail*, trans Evans

[4] *From Ritual To Romance*, Jessie L. Weston (Cambridge University Press, 1920)

[5] *Perlesvaus*, Williams

It (Not It)

There are no words
to contain It,

even the Word that was
with It and was It

in the beginning
before words were.

The boundless finger
pointing at Itself. (Or No Self)

Still, myriad names and forms
to furnish the suspicion that somewhere

in there, which is everywhere and nowhere,
is something like a personality

working to perfect Itself
in us, our bit of ‘It is with us’.

Only, taken literally, even
a Personal Avatar has been known

to divide us from It, and It
from Itself. (From No Self)

The wonder of it is:
we are It

sensing and sensed. Here to know
and love Itself

in us and through us and
for us to receive and amplify

love and gratitude and to
share It around,

knowing that if It's me
It must be you too.

We're All It. Nothing of It
that's not It. So

feel free to be It and call it
as you will, according to

your place in It. When I'm so
deep in It, I am It, deep in trance,

I call It 'Baby'. It calls
Itself. (Its No Self) Says:

'Baby,
let's dance.'

Prayer to The Other

Grant me the grace
          to hold this space
to let your presence shine,

show to me
          your secret face
and I will show you mine.

Benignus and The Bards

One bright morning in late August I chance upon Pok the Bard outside St Benedict's, just down the road from my place. The church was originally dedicated to St Benignus, an Irish companion of St Patrick, though the namers may have confused him with Beon the Hermit.

William of Malmesbury reports that Benignus lived as a hermit in the village of Meare around 460 AD. In 901 his relics were transferred by boat for reburial at Glastonbury Abbey. As the boat docked a rainbow appeared in the sky, spanning The Abbey. The reliquary was opened and one of the bones used to make the sign of the cross over the crowd, unleashing torrents of miraculous cures and other signs of Divine grace. His church was built close to the landing stage where the saint's relics came ashore.

By the 13th century it stood on Grope Cunt Lane, in the profane town beyond the sacred precinct of The Abbey. There's a hole in one side of the porch through which lepers used to reach to beg for alms from the congregation. These days on Thursdays the church serves a free lunch to the street-people and anyone who cares to show up – as much for the social as for the meal. We sit in the churchyard supping soup and sharing news. Claire the volunteer gardener is a vital hub in our self-help network.

A descendant of the Holy Thorn grows in the churchyard, which has become a sacred space for me to hold discreet Vigils. On the wild night of 23rd March I'd stood facing the West Door, watched by sculpted saints and gargoyles, asking the spirits to open the pathways.

Pok points across the road to Number 30 Benedict Street where he once lived with his band, The Space Goats. It's the former site of Gino's Cafe, where John Michell and Harry Fainlight once traumatised a lorry driver whilst plotting the Avalonian Renaissance.

When Pok and I met in 1999 at *The Warp* parties, we bonded as brothers, self-styled Bards using psychedelics as sacraments to commune with The Otherworlds, each following our calling to serve our personal Muse, Spirit Guide or Divinity. I was deep into my John Crow magical workings with The Goose; Pok was dedicated to his vision of the Divine Feminine expressed in poetry, music and eco-activism. At Twyford Down and in many other actions and occupations he'd embraced his identity as a Bard dedicated to protecting the Earth and her creatures.

We were often on the same bill in the Conscious Party scene, playing the same Bedouin tents in festivals. We even did three gigs together in Ron Tree's band, The Mother of All Bands.

During my first long winter in Glastonbury, I'd sometimes walk out to the Morlands travellers' site at Beckery to look for Pok, Snakes or Anette. They were never home, but I'd often run into him. One crisp February afternoon, he led me on a walk through the fields to the south of Wearyall Hill. The traffic-noise faded until there was only the wind and the distant cries of birds. He shared how much he'd suffered for his art and vision, and how he hoped his fortunes were about to change. I encouraged him to keep the faith and trust in the Unfolding.

As the town opened up in summer, our chance encounters became more frequent. One of us would find the other singing or performing poetry in one of the buskers' alcoves on the High Street. He looked increasingly pained and stressed. One day I gave him street-therapy, letting him share his troubles and then singing him healing songs.

Pok is following his poetic calling with utter conviction. His life is chaotic and precarious. He spent last winter in a caravan on the rat-infested travellers' site at Morlands with only the most basic comforts. He complains about the traffic fumes when he busks on the High Street. And, sooner or later, he gets on to the tricky Matter of being The Bard of Ynys Witrin.

We've seen how the Grail legends draw on ancient oral traditions transmitted by legendary Celtic Bards. Although transcribed in medieval times, the works attributed to Taliesin, Aneirin and Myrddin evoke an earlier age of semi-divine heroes and their quests for the Cauldron of Inspiration.

In the *Hanes Taliesin*, The Bard 'of the radiant brow' is born of a shamanistic initiation. He starts out as Gwion Bach, the simple village boy charged with tending the Cauldron of Ceridwen as she brews a magic potion intended for her son. Three drops of scalding liquid splash onto Gwion's thumb; he sucks it and… He knows all there is to know, not least that the angry Goddess is hell-bent on his destruction. There follows an extraordinary shape-shifting sequence. He changes into a hare, a fish, a bird, a grain of wheat. Ceridwen gives chase as a hound, a hawk, an otter, and finally the hen who pecks up the grain. Gwion undergoes a final transformation in her womb, to be reborn as Taliesin, the all-knowing Bard.

After the Roman occupation of these islands and the slaughter of The Druids, the Bardic lineages were driven underground. Their traditions survived in Ireland, Wales and the West of England, where they nurtured the emergence of a distinctive Celtic Christianity.

A dim echo of the Bardic voice survived in the Welsh Eisteddfods, in a relatively unbroken tradition going back to the Middle Ages. It was revitalised by a renewed interest in Druidism initiated by 17th century antiquarians like John Audley and William Stukeley, then developed by mavericks like Edward Williams (Iolo Morganwg) who devised a new *Gorsedd* or *Gorsedh* held on London's Primrose Hill, and by more conservative organisations like the United Order of Druids which began as a gentleman's club. In 1858 the Welsh National Eisteddfod featured 'The *Gorsedd* of the Bards of the Isle of Britain'.

The contemporary revival took shape in 1964 when Ross Nichols inaugurated The Order of Bards, Ovates and Druids. In the 1990s Tim Sebastian of the Secular Order of Druids (SOD) began reinstating the Bardic Chairs of Albion. Glastonbury's own *Gorsedh Ynys Witrin* was established in 1995 by Arch-Druids Dreow Bennett and Denny Michell the Mayor of Glastonbury, with Tim Hall chaired as its first Bard.

The Bard is elected at an annual *Gorsedh*, in which prospective Bards compete with poems on a particular theme and the assembly votes to decide who wins the Chair. The Bard then holds the post for a year. They're expected to perform civic and ceremonial duties, to encourage others to learn the Bardic Way and, at the end of their tenure, to set the theme for the competition to elect their successor. Exactly how these duties are performed, and how seriously they're taken, is very much up to the individual incumbent.

Pok takes his responsibilities intensely seriously, as sacred duties intrinsic to his very being. The previous two *Gorsedhs* were cancelled during the pandemic lockdown, so he's now in his third year of being Bard. It weighs heavily on him.

So now, by St Benignus church, Pok's consciousness is streaming. He wants to scrap the competition, bring back the street-bards, reclaim the Bardic tradition from the Bardic College, 'elevate the Cup over the Chair' and generally 'throw down the gauntlet'! (In Time, having used me as a sounding-board, he'll change his tune – or fine-tune it – but that's a whole other tale!)

A few days later I come upon Pok and Tim Raven by the Abbey Gate. They're sat on the wall close to the huge pieces of broken masonry that remind me of dragon's teeth. With a dramatic flourish, Pok throws his 'gauntlet' at my feet: it's a sprig of oak-leaves. I pick it up, cradle it like a baby bird, then offer it to Raven, who accepts with a chuckle: 'a Conspiracy of Ravens.' We agree to put on our own Bardic show, an alternative *Gorsedd* with Pok, Raven, Crow and...

Ash the Destroyer has to be in on it too. We've journeyed together through many a night sharing poems, songs and stories around camp-fires. At the Wilderness Festival, he'd fixed it for him, Pok and me to host a bad-boy *Gorsedd* on the edge of festie-town, performing with hill-billy metal bands and burlesque dancers. During Glastonbury's dark days, Ash had kept the faith for the street-bards. He'd even tried to initiate a *Gorsedd* to be held on the eight spokes of the Wheel of the Year at St Ben's, but back then the vicar had got the wind up and slammed the door.

We affirm that now the time is right and that St Ben's is the place for us. The church-warden Liz is friendly and direct and very 'can do'. I've already sounded her out about performing in the church. Now Pok calls Liz and gets an encouraging response.

Next Sunday, we 'take Pok to church'. (Our little joke.) Though pagan to the core, Katy and I have come to love the Love at the heart of the Christian Mysteries. Pok likes to wind up Christians, telling them how he was with Jeshua in the beginning – and shared a bong with him. A claim worthy of Taliesin!

This Sunday it's Celtic Communion in St Ben's conducted by the Revd. Diana Dingles, the 'Fairy Goth Vicar'. Diana has a dispensation to enter into dialogue with other faiths, which in Glastonbury means pagans and New Agers of all persuasions. Her service reflects the urge to reconnect Christian worship with Nature. There are no Creeds, not even a Lord's Prayer, and I receive the communion wafer without any of the reservations I sometimes feel in church.

After the service, Katy and I are chilling back home when there's a tap on the window. It's Pok, wired and sparking. We sit in the garden. He tells us how he wants to 'leave a great smoking crater in Avalon'.

I say he has to be pure, like Perceval, empty of ulterior motives. To do it for the *craic*, for the joy of doing it, not to cock a snook at the Bardic College or to start a new War of The Bards. To trip light and caper.

An hour in the garden, after much mental jousting, we've sketched out the basic shape of an alternative *Gorsedd*. I play Practical John, reminding him we've a show to put on. We need a running order, some ground-rules.

So… Two rounds. Each Bard gets two sets of seven minutes. If we overrun our slot then Pok gets to poke us back into the fold with his staff, his Ox-poke.

The Ox-poke is one of my left-field ideas, along with our show title borrowed from Taliesin's poem, his satire on those who would compete for his Chair:

The Ox-Pen of the Bards.

Pok likes it. It chimes with his call for The Bards to dirty their hands in the shit of the market-place.

On 19th September, the night of the Full Moon, Harvest Moon, and Autumn Equinox, The Bards gather in the church of St Benignus. Pok arrives with three marrows, which we symbolically place around our altar to represent the three bars of Awen. He raises his poke.

Seamus his bearer holds up a banner with the Awen symbol, and we all shout: 'Hail the Bard!'

And we're on.

The Ox-Pen of The Bards

Pok, thrice Bard of Ynys Witrin
fling down the gauntlet; this Gorsedd
feather and take flight

to light among the ravens on the tower
here at St Ben's,'Benign Us', in these Twelve Hides:
The Ox-Pen of the Bards.

Here let Pok wield the Poke of Taliesin,
and when we brag and bellow and bang on
then let Pok poke us back into the Pen.

For we are not come to lock horns
over who be Prize Bull, but to sing our Taliesin
in many tongues and fluid genders.

To sing the ancient trackways back to being; track back
to primal drum and word of breath; the pattern
of the stars
and their imprint in our living Grail Earth.

To raise the bar for Each in the Other; practice
the Art of Vision, and the craft: form, rhythm,
the feathering of words to fly

beyond. To rig the Good Ship Prydwyn
and set sail to raid the Cauldron
for three precious drops of pure Awen.

To sing our Taliesin and his dark mother Ceridwen
snuffling along Her Great Sow's Way
to farrow by the Old Church apple tree [1]

in these Twelve Hides:

our Ox-Pen of The Bards.

[1] Joseph was granted the Twelve Hides and The Old Church was built by him, or by God. The town has its own founding legend. Glasteing, the last of twelve brothers, is said to have followed a wandering sow along the Sugewege (Sow's Way) to Glastonbury where he found her suckling her litter under an apple tree by the Old Church. The sow is a totem animal of The Goddess Ceridwen, the mother of Taliesin.

The Witch and Taliesin

The Witch she says to Backward Boy:
'Stir that pot!
Make a potion for my Ugly Boy.
Show him what's what!
But if you know what's good for you,
Don't drink one drop!'
Backward Boy he grins at her,
Says he: 'Why not?'

The Witch she says to Backward Boy:
'Don't get fresh!
This brew is for my Ugly Boy
My own blood and flesh.
Belladonna, henbane
And a pinch of witches' yeast
To teach my son to speak in tongues
With all the birds and beasts!'

Awake, wake, wake the snake, three times three.
Awake, wake, wake the snake, three times three.
Awake, wake, wake the snake, three times three.
Shake it till it shift its shape and let it wake in me.

Backward Boy he tend the fire
And trust his luck!
Cauldron hubble-bubble, spit out
Three boiling drops.
Backward Boy says 'Ow!'
And give his thumb a big suck.
Then all the birds are singing.
And then all the singing stops.

And the birds say: ‘Witch is coming, boy,
You better beware!’
Backward Boy he shift his shape
He turn into a hare.
But now the witch is giving chase,
She hunt him as a hound.
She run him three times round the world.
She run that hare to ground.

So he jump into the river
And he turn into a fish,
But she dive in as an otter,
And now he’s her tasty dish.
He crawl out on the dry land
And he turn into a seed,
But she turn into a chicken
And she peck him up for feed.

Awake, wake, wake the snake, three times three.
Awake, wake, wake the snake, three times three.
Awake, wake, wake the snake, three times three.
Shake it till it shift its shape and let it wake in me.

And once again I shift my shape
In the Witch’s womb.
Now I am as old as Time, I shine
In the sun and the stars and the moon.
The one who Death did not destroy.
Who knows where I begin?
I used to be the Backward Boy
But now I’m Taliesin.

Awake, wake, wake the snake, three times three.
Awake, wake, wake the snake, three times three.
Awake, wake, wake the snake, three times three.
Shake it till it shift its shape and let it wake in me.

I used to be the Backward Boy
But now I’m Taliesin.

In the 1920s the American sculptor and esotericist Katharine Maltwood was commissioned to create a map to illustrate the English translation of *The High History of The Holy Grail*. The idea was to track the adventures of Arthur and his knights in Somerset.

In the course of their quest the knights sometimes have to defeat fearsome lions who guard the pathways and castle gates. Maltwood was staring at an Ordnance Survey map of the Somerton area when the outline of a lion traced by the River Cary suddenly leapt out at her. The adjacent Dundon and Lollover hills seemed to form the shape of a baby. An astrologer friend suggested that these could be gigantic representations of the star-signs for Leo and Gemini.

In her books – *Glastonbury's Temple of the Stars*, *Enchantments of Britain* and the photographic *Ariel Survey* – Maltwood unpacks her vision of a huge landscaped zodiac, mapped out with giant effigies representing the twelve star-signs processing in a circle. When a planisphere is superimposed to scale on her map, the constellations of the zodiac are seen to fit precisely over their respective earth-worked symbols. She envisions a vast instrument used for astronomical and astrological calculations, constructed by Sumer-Chaldean priests in 2,700 BC.

Taking *The High History* as a solar myth, Maltwood identifies its heroes with the four seasons and specific zodiac signs. By linking selected incidents from their quest with physical features on her landscaped Zodiac, she claims to have discovered the actual form and true meaning of Merlin's Round Table,

Taliesin's Caer Sidi, the cauldron of Annwn. The key to unlock *The High History* and to reveal The Holy Grail!

Academics from many disciplines were quick to dismiss Maltwood's theory and its shaky foundations. Linguists derided her ignorance of etymology, the way she conflated roots of words and derivations of homonyms. Grail scholars objected that *The High History*'s astrological symbols could be decoded without a physical zodiac. They noted how her selective reading left out huge tracts of the original narrative, including crucial episodes that invited alternative interpretations. Ordinance Survey experts pointed out how easy it was to draw similar images on any aerial photograph, and how some of the lines of her images were traced with roads, fields or other man-made features that did not exist back in 2700 BC!

At the time of her death in 1961, her life's work was largely forgotten – or archived as a delightfully crackpot theory. The Glastonbury renaissance of the 1970s reawakened serious interest in her Zodiac. In *The View Over Atlantis* John Michell credits her, along with William Stukeley and Alfred Watkins, as being one of his predecessors in the rediscovery of megalithic science and Earth Mysteries. In his later works he presents a more considered view:

… the weak point of Maltwood's vision was her literal expression of it. Many of her effigies seem random and ill-defined and best classified as "simulacra", examples of the tendency in nature and the human eye, working together, to create apparent symbols and living forms in clouds, rocks and

landscapes. Yet through those effigies she created a powerful image, infectious to the imagination, and effective in awakening twentieth-century perception of the large-scale, geomantic works of the ancients.[1]

Her leading apostle Mary Caine published *The Glastonbury Zodiac*, expanding on Maltwood's esoteric theories. She recognises that the Zodiac is essentially natural, though shaped and refined by human works – roads, paths, canals – and suggests that questions as to who made it or whether it was consciously constructed to a grand design:

… miss the whole point – which is to recognise that Nature works to a pattern. The first civilised men undoubtedly recognised this. They realised that this pattern operated not only on matter but on Time: that it was in fact a Space-Time pattern.[2]

The poet in Caine enables her to unlock Maltwood's mystical vision, to explore the Zodiac not as a means to explain everything, but as a portal to an initiation, to experience the underlying unity of mind and matter, Eternity and Time.

In his introduction to Mary Caine's book, Geoffrey Ashe commends her for moving away from the 'pseudo-archaeological' and 'towards the psychological and spiritual…'

Is the Zodiac literally there or not? … My own feeling is that is is not there as, say, the Egyptian pyramids are, but that is not the whole story… I am reminded of the Rorschach ink-blot test, or of seeing pictures in the fire. People see what they are attuned to see… What matters is the experience of those who do see them – the wide-ranging meditations which they can conjure up.[3]

This being Glastonbury, even in the 2020s AD, there are those who believe that The Star Temple was literally created in 2700 BC by the people of The Summer Lands. And who's to say they're wrong? The scientific establishment may have exposed Maltwood's unscientific methodology, but no one has conclusively disproved her theory. If it helps some believers to see the star-signs revealed in the landscape, the Heavens reflected on Earth, who are we to deny them? In my book, any vision that connects us with the Earth and the stars is holy.

The trouble with literalism is that it tends to close minds. It can make us believe that The Round Table, Caer Sidi and The Grail can all be neatly wrapped up in a single paradigm. The key to The Mysteries becomes the lock, the block. Our new model or description of The Grail becomes a substitute, an obstruction to our experience of The Grail itself.

The Poetic Vision is not be confused with make believe. Our thoughts can take on an autonomous life on The Astral, which can, in turn, shape our perception of the world. It is precisely this mutual resonance ('As Above So Below') which allows magical practitioners to re-pattern consensual reality, its maps and models, the material world itself. So when I speak of the Poetic Vision I do not imply that it is inferior to the reality underpinned by empirical science. When we engage imaginatively with the Maltwood-Caine patterning we can use it to journey, to enter the portal towards which the Zodiac can only point the way.

In my own small world, in a past life, I had a direct experience of how a vision can create a new pattern, changing the identity of a physical place. The place was Cross Bones Graveyard, which The Goose had revealed as Her burial ground. As a result of our 23-year magical work, Cross Bones now exists in this world, and on The Astral, as The Outcasts' Graveyard.

The site-owners had been looking to redevelop the site. They commissioned a report to try to prove that Cross Bones was not the same 'Single Women's churchyard' referred to by John Stow in 1598.

By which time we'd created our shrine to the outcast dead. As John Crow said at the Vigil: 'If it wasn't then, it is now!'

And so it was. Now it's a Garden of Remembrance.

And so it is with Katharine Maltwood. At the very least she made an extraordinary intuitive leap to see what no-one had seen before, re-patterning the Somerset landscape to evoke her Star Temple.

If it wasn't there in 2700 BC, it is now.

[1] John Michell, *New Light on the Ancient Mystery of Glastonbury*
[2] Mary Caine, *The Glastonbury Giants or Zodiac*, essay in *Glastonbury, Ancient Avalon, New Jerusalem* (ed. Anthony Roberts)
[3] Geoffrey Ashe, introduction to *The Glastonbury Zodiac* by Mary Caine

Thanks to Katharine Maltwood and Mary Caine for reinstating *Maggoty Paggoty* as an ancient site dedicated to the Mother Goddess (Ma) and Father God (Pa).

Human Rites

Turn the body round, m'lovers,
Turn the body round.
Raise it in the sky, then
Lay it on the ground.

In the Earth then let it lie
Nine month long to putrefy, then
Raise it up again, m'lovers,
Raise it up again.

Turn the body round, m'lovers,
Turn the body round.
In the Dark and Light, then
In the Sight and Sound.

Scatter it in spring-time seed,
Give to water and to feed, then
Raise it up again, m'lovers,
Raise it up again.

In rags, in bags, in straw, in sack.
The price of a penny is all we lack.
On a twisty track we go clickity-clackity
Home and back to Maggoty Paggoty.

Ancestor Souls

The Ox-Pen of The Bards marked our first full year of living in Glastonbury. From then on, late September and through October, I found myself tuning into familiar markers of the changing seasons.

In the Abbey grounds, willow, lime, chestnut, maple, ginkgo, aglow: pale yellow, russet, flaming scarlet, bright gold. In the orchard the apples redden and ripen, the trees weighed down with their bounty, calling me back from reverie as a windfall apple crunches underfoot.

On Wednesday afternoons, the Hare Krishnas serve street curry and rice by the Celtic Cross outside St John's Church. The Krishnas have embraced feeding people as a devotional act, as integral to their practice as chanting the names of the Divine. It's a good test for any belief-system: does it balance the quest for personal gnosis with simple acts of love and kindness?

In the food queue I meet Jenny Bliss-Bennett. She's wearing a onesie. We've heard of one another, and had heard each other play at the Paddington Farm festival in September. Although we hadn't spoken then, I'd been touched by her eclectic singing. She introduces me to her partner Will; they play in a well-known local band, Queen Space Baroque. And by the time we've finished our free food – Hare Krishna! - we've arranged to have a jam and recording session.

On the agreed night I show up at their place. We improvise, Jenny singing and playing keyboards and violin, Will on guitar and synthesizer, with me reciting incantations from my work-in-progress, my little Grail Cycle. Nothing is planned, but as we go deeper into the zone, the words and music mesh in unexpected ways. Jenny is a virtuoso instrumentalist, and her high, spooky child-woman voice scales the celestial heights. Will conjures up ethereal soundscapes. I'm reciting in trance, hearing the words and seeing the spiritual forms they invoke.

An enchantment is cast.

Jenny has booked the Library of Avalon for their Halloween concert. It's hidden away in the innermost courtyard of the Glastonbury Experience, a stone and wood-beam lodge stacked with esoteric books. Queen Space Baroque did a livestreamed concert there last Halloween – during lockdown so there was no audience. She asks if I'd like to perform with them this time. I'd been contemplating doing my own Halloween ritual in St Ben's. In no time we've agreed that we'll do a ritual concert together.

Ancestor Souls is born.

A week before the concert my friend Claudia, the theatre-maker and fearless psychonaut, died.

Throughout our 42-year friendship Claudia was loving, generous, intensely loyal and unflinchingly honest – an exemplar to anyone seeking to live an authentic life. She always egged me on to push my boundaries and supported my experimental writing and performances. She was on the original *Mysteries Pilgrimage* – when I took our writers' group on an esoteric tour of Southwark, outlining my then new work-in-progress which drew on the history of The Liberty of the Clink and the Winchester Geese. At the after-walk debrief, it was Claudia who kept telling me: 'Don't forget those Geese! They're the key.' And it was she who gave me the bottle of liquid acid that helped raise The Goose Spirit and fuelled my visionary nights at the end of the last millennium.

During this first year in Glastonbury, I've invoked The Goose to mediate in my interactions with local spirits of place. But this is the first time I've publicly conducted Her Halloween ritual. And now, tonight is charged with Claudia – her absence and presence. Claudia, who gave me the key to unlock The Goose, presiding over our work with the spirits tonight.

The Library of Avalon is tiny. We manage to seat sixteen paying guests, and that's a full house. With performers, front-of-house staff and guests we're twenty-three, the Number of The Goose.

It's a concert within a ritual within a journey within a concert – and so to infinity! A journey in mind and spirit, a vision journey with Astral music and magical incantations.

In these islands, we say that on All Hallows Eve 'the veil is thin'. We commune with the spirits of the dead, the Ancestors, with friends or family on the Other Side, and with all spiritual agencies who join us in our work of healing and transformation.

As we journey deeper into ritual space, we see there is no veil! There are no dead. There are no 'sides'. There is only an infinite inter-connected network of light, energy, consciousness, unfolding in shining emptiness...

Samhain

Here, the veil between the worlds
dissolves:

the living, the dead
share the brew, break the bread.

Ancestor souls
converse and commune,

this Samhain night,
by the light of a bone-

white

moon.

Re-membering Richard Whiting

St John's Church, 14th November 2021. On the stroke of four o'clock we stand for a minute's silence in remembrance of Richard Whiting, the last Abbot of Glastonbury Abbey. The Abbey was the last Somerset monastery to resist Henry VIII's 'Dissolution'. On 15th November 1539, Abbot Whiting and two of his monks, John Thorne and Roger James, were hung, drawn and quartered on Glastonbury Tor.

There are twenty or thirty of us gathered by Bligh Bond's Celtic memorial cross. There's local psycho-geographer Paul Weston, Angela the transpersonal mystic who's recently taken to wearing a black veil and medieval plague-doctor's beak to enhance her trance-states, and Amanda, the single Mum and irresistible force for God who started the petition for a Royal Pardon for Abbot Whiting.

This act of remembrance has been called by Jon Cousins, the Mayor of Glastonbury. Our Mayor is a mystic, steeped in local esoteric lore. Tomorrow is the official 482nd anniversary of Whiting's judicial murder, but today is Remembrance Sunday and new research leaked by The Mayor suggests the atrocity was actually committed on 14th November.

Jon tells how Whiting's limbs were scattered far and wide, exhibited in Bath, Wells, Bridgwater, Ilchester; his head was nailed over the Great North Gate of the Abbey. He speaks movingly of how the literal dismemberment of Whiting's body was also an act of metaphysical violence designed to dismember the spiritual corpus of 'Glaston', which we are now here to 're-member'.

This chimes with my works with The Goose as a channel of Isis, who traversed Egypt, gathering the scattered body-parts of her beloved Osiris then literally 're-membering' him.

Jon leads us into Silver Street to the site of the former North Gate, now a small arch with an iron-barred gate looking onto the Abbey ruins. We each place a white rose on the gate. Claire the St Ben's church gardener has brought a bottle of holy water from Prinknash Abbey. Whiting's bones were discreetly ferried away, first to Caldey then Prinknash in Gloucestershire, where they remain to this day, revered as Holy Relics. The Mayor tells us that he himself was fortunate to visit Prinknash and to make an act of reverence to them. Or as Paul Weston had confided to me, with his characteristic Essex-boy directness: 'Jon got to kiss Whiting's bones!'

Jon pours the holy water on the gate, a simple act with complex reverberations. We stand in silence.

The following morning, 15th November, the 'official' date of Whiting's martyrdom, a small crowd gathers in the ruined Quire of the Abbey. The surviving arched walls and the great broken arches of the bell-tower are ghostly in the mist. At the eleventh hour, Paul Weston reads the names of the Glastonbury Abbots, ending with Richard Whiting.

Mayor Jon Cousins then stands behind the High Altar. He shows where psychic archaeologist Frederick Bligh Bond dug up bones by the High Altar. Bligh Bond used automatic writing to contact his spiritual guides, the monks of The Company of Avalon, to ask whose bones they were. The monks replied that they were the bones of Richard Whiting.

The Mayor of Glastonbury tells how, having written his pamphlet *Remember Richard Whiting*, he was invited to Prinknash Abbey and permitted to venerate the bones, an intensely spiritual and emotional experience. Afterwards, the Benedictine monk made Jon a cup of tea in his cell, and confided: 'There is nothing in your pamphlet with which we disagree.' Jon later meditated on what he'd said, and realised that the 'we' referred to the Benedictine Order. This is remarkable, given Jon's radical suggestion that Whiting was hacked to bits in a ritual act of desecration.

I feel honoured and humbled to be invited to join Paul and Jon in this triadic act of restitution. I do *A Little Spell of Unforgetting*, my first Glastonbury poem, inspired by the ruined Abbey and my propitious meeting with Paul in the Edgar Chapel at last year's Blake celebration. It invokes 'the Time of the Remembering' in which Glastonbury's spiritual agencies come together in an act of healing and restoration.

Two weeks later, we're back in the Edgar Chapel to celebrate William Blake's 264th Birthday. Last year we were seven; now we're twenty-eight, a four-fold increase. The Blakean printer Peter Fraser reminds us of Blake's 'four-fold Vision'.

The Mayor reiterates the choice facing us here and now: Jerusalem versus the Dark Satanic Mills. Paul Weston segues into observing that, whilst Blake invokes the spiritual forms of the other English

Cathedrals and Dioceses, the spiritual heart of England is never once mentioned in *Jerusalem* or any of his works. Paul suggests this is because Glastonbury, and specifically The Abbey, is the living embodiment of Jerusalem itself!

We stand in a circle, taking turns to recite from the works of The Master. Our Blake happenings are already taking on their own quirky conventions. The science fiction and fantasy author Liz Williams does a bit of bibliomancy, opening the *Complete Works* to read at random. Last time it was Blake's dark musings on 'the Vegetative Female'. Today we get one of his letters to Thomas Butts. As Liz paraphrases it: 'I haven't done your stuff, shit happened, sorry about that, moreover I don't know when you'll get your stuff, but it will turn up eventually and anyway, Eternity! And my Vision!'

As the host, I aim to keep it informal, to facilitate whatever the attendees wish to offer, something from Blake or a poem, song or testimony of their own. Maybe I get too relaxed, become sloppy and careless. Aware that we're standing on the Dod Line, I perform *Dod Cut The Cards,* but fluff the first line of the third verse and momentarily forget the second line. Then, leading the 'congregation' in a rousing rendition of *Jerusalem,* I somehow switch the second and third lines (replacing 'Walk upon England's pastures green' with 'And did the Holy Lamb of God') thereby throwing myself and everyone else into confusion.

Afterwards everyone seems to be in good spirits; I garner lots of compliments and positive feedback. Even Katy, who can be my sternest critic, remarks how well I facilitated the event 'without getting in the way'. Then a woman I'd met on the way in to The Abbey takes me to task for my blunder during the singing of *Jerusalem.* She urges me to accept that I made a serious mistake and makes me repeat the correct lines, three times. I see it's well-meant, and resist the defensive urge to dismiss her as yet another Lightworker looking to lay their trip on me. I do as she says and thank her for the correction.

Jon Cousins asks if Katy and I would like to come for a coffee and 'a chat about London and Glastonbury'. Still high on performance adrenaline, I anticipate a merry hour affirming each other's work and discovering deep connections. And, in a way all that happens too, though not at all as I expected.

It soon becomes clear that Jon is preoccupied by the mistakes I made during the celebration. I try to shrug them off: maybe I'm getting old and losing my once prodigious memory – but hey, it's not like it was a High Church Ritual; just an impromptu celebration. I'm not going to lose sleep over fluffing a couple of lines.

Jon's having none of it, darkly hinting that others had noted what happened there: 'This isn't London. This is Glastonbury. If you're going to stand on the Dod Line as John Crow then you have to play the part. Because, whatever you think or say, it's a ceremony. Others will see it like that, as a ritual act, and if something goes wrong, and it certainly did…'

He takes me back to when I forgot the second and third lines of the third verse of my own poem, pressing me to repeat them. I do, this time correctly, and suddenly see what he's getting at:

Then the deck get stacked; the message get scrambled
The Hanged Man strung up on The Tor.

This is not any old poem. It's a specific spell, for healing and restoration, cast on highly-charged sacred ground. In short, John Crow was standing on the Dod Line, naming the ritual sacrifice once made to appease the Dark Powers and to destroy the very fabric of Glaston itself!

Jon is in no doubt: 'You flagged yourself up! You were noticed! They saw you and what you were doing. It's no accident that you forgot those specific lines. "The message get scrambled"? They were using your own words against you. They deliberately intervened to distract and confuse you.'

Jon keeps apologising; he doesn't want to seem disrespectful or presumptuous, but... It gradually dawns that he's gently warning me I'm in out of my depth. We spend the next seven hours unpacking it, going deep into what our mutual friend Paul calls Deep Glastonbury. How Glaston is a spirit or thought-form superimposed on the ancient sacred landscape. How we are here to build Jerusalem, where the Male and the Female, IESUS MARIA, are harmonised in The Temple of Reconciliation. And how there are those who wish only to destroy.

It surrounds surreal, coming from The Mayor, but this is Glastonbury and I question neither his sincerity nor his sanity. Katy and I make cups of tea as he shares his personal journey. He came to Glastonbury to set up a Time Bank. He was working late in his office in Richard Whiting House in Silver Street when he heard a disembodied voice say 'Remember Richard Whiting.'

And not once, but many times over the nights to come. Back then, Jon didn't even know who Abbot Whiting was. When he found out he was appalled – not only by the vile act of dismemberment, but by dimly glimpsing the magnitude of the esoteric work that he (Jon) was called to undertake.

The 'Re-membering'.

Jon began receiving vast downloads of information, seemingly manifested by otherworldly guides. Things started to go badly wrong in his life. His relationship broke up. He seriously wondered if he was losing his mind. He asked the guides for some proof of their reality. They replied with playful demonstrations of synchronicity, arranging for him to visit a man he'd never met who then delivered a message that unambiguously confirmed their existence.

It gets better – and worse! Jon is struck down with pneumonia and can't get treatment. In a delirious vision he asks to be shown his enemies. The vision morphs into a Sergeant Pepper cover, hyper-real with the figures like cut-outs in a 3D landscape; and substituting for the Beatles are the Seymours, Henry VIII's brother-in-law and his sinister kin. Jon can examine them in detail but the figures behind them are murky, swathed in fog. He asks to be shown who they are. The fog clears and he sees they're him and all the people he knows in Glastonbury. We're 'Them.'

I listen carefully to all he says, knowing it's important and (somewhere on the other side of Reason) True. At the same time I take care not to attach to anything he says, especially with reference to the Dark Powers who had apparently clocked my poetic intervention on The Dod Line and hit back with scrambled verses. As I've said, it's all too easy to feed that which we fear.

But it must have played on my mind. The next day in the bathroom, drying after a shower, I'm overcome by the enormity of what Jon had said. I feel a dizzying terror – here's me and Jon and Pok and Paul and a motley crew of poets, psychics and guardians up against Inhuman Forces who stage-managed the ritual sacrifice of Richard Whiting and have manipulated our history ever since. What have we got against that?

And, instantaneously, I hear my own voice answering myself out loud: 'We've got Jesus. And Mary, Mother of God. The Magdalene. The Goose! We've got Blake! We've got IESUS-MARIA!'

At that exact moment a shaft of sunlight breaks through the window flooding me with light.

Jon dropped round to ours next day with the three pamphlets he'd promised me.[1] They provide the context and sources for his suggestion that Whiting's judicial murder was part of an act of desecration, to create a market-place in the heart of the very Temple:

In 1189, Glaston's sacred precinct – originally the whole peninsula – was redefined. Inside the new precinct, the holy symbolism of IESUS remained intact, but it was not so for MARIA. The Queen of Heaven was symbolically split apart. Aspects of MARIA, the Mother of God and Blessed Virgin, remained inside. But Mary's Bride aspect, The Magdalene, was consciously removed and placed outside – where we find Magdalene Street, and the Magdalene Chapel and Almshouses! […] *This corrupt paradigm was enhanced by the introduction – at the end of Magdalene Street – of the marketplace.* […] *The ultimate debasement of the Feminine* […] *compounded by the introduction of licensed prostitution just off Magdalene Street, in the aptly named Cock Lane and Grope Cunt Lane!* [1]

I'm again struck by the resonances with my own work. *The Southwark Mysteries* and *The Ballad of Grope Cunt Lane* explore this same dichotomy of Spirit and flesh, Sacred and profane.

Jon's third pamphlet entertains the notion that the leaden cross identifying 'Arthur's Grave' in The Abbey was a medieval decoy, placed there to distract from the final resting-place of Mary, mother of Jesus. In this version Joseph of Arimathea brings Mary to Her Glastonbury sanctuary, 'a place prepared of God', to protect Her from The Destroyer, the Dragon in The Book of Revelation who threatens the woman clothed with the sun, the moon and the stars. Of course the Dragon has many aspects and interpretations. In my own work here, I invoke the Dragon Lines of the Earth Energies, tempered and guided by Mary and Michael. One vision does not negate the other, indeed they are classic Blakean 'Contraries'. Appropriate then that I'd initiated our Blake celebration that morning with a quote from *The Marriage of Heaven and Hell*:

Without Contraries is no progression.

And how apposite that I should have met two friends and allies in The Great Work exactly a year apart – Paul Weston last year and Jon Cousins today – at William Blake's Birthday bash in Glastonbury Abbey!

[1] *The Glastonbury Documents: III. The Temple of Reconciliation.* Jon F. Cousins, available from Glastonbury Information Centre

Pomparles[1]

When it's me
laid down bloodied
and chill in the damp moss, falling
between worlds.

Grant me the strength
for one last heft to hurl mine own
ex-calibrated sword, the gift
returned to The Giver.

And not rely
on grieving friends to do the parting
act that must be done before
I fully live – and die.

For knowing when to surrender your power,
when you're strong enough
to choose it, is key
as knowing when to take and use it.

[1] Pomparles Bridge derives its name from the *Pons Perilis*, the 'perilous bridge' over the river Brue to the south-west of Glastonbury. Even in John Cowper Powys' time, the Brue was a sluggish stream choked with refuse. Yet it is here that his John Crow glimpses Arthur's sword 'shearing the sun-lit air' and 'falling into the mud of the river'. For this is the place from which Arthur is said to have returned his sword to the feminine power embodied in The Lady of the Lake.

Not The End

As a young psychonaut of the early 1970s I was impressed by Carlos Casteneda's books charting his supposed initiation by the Yaqui sorcerer Don Juan into the use of plant teachers and other techniques for altering consciousness. The veracity of Casteneda's work was subsequently challenged and his books discreetly moved from 'anthropology' to the 'fiction' shelves of bookshops and libraries. Yet even if Don Juan only existed in Casteneda's over-active inner life, the teachings themselves, delivered in a punchy, accessible, colloquial manner, carry the authentic voice of a practising magician. I was particularly struck by Don Juan's instruction to use Death as an 'advisor', to imagine our own Death standing beside us waiting to tap us on the shoulder. I've often used it as a practical technique to exorcise the petty concerns that preoccupy my mind. My friend Di reckons I've been rehearsing my death ever since I was 17. Certainly my teenage psychedelic initiations had something of a 'little death' about them, a dissolving of boundaries and the sense that I was only an ephemeral manifestation of an eternal, infinite consciousness.

In January 1979 I almost got myself killed twice in two days, trekking in the Himalayas. As my Danish companion and I were heading up to Annapurna Base Camp, we experienced a complete white-out. Unable to see him, I was following his footprints. I suddenly lost my footing and found myself half-buried in snow. I saw flashes of violet light, my body suffused in a warm glow, and imagined myself lying in the snow, at peace. Then some atavistic survival urge

shocked me out of my complacency, reminding me that I was showing symptoms of altitude sickness and hypothermia and that if I didn't get up I'd be dead in an hour. I staggered to my feet and lumbered after the fast-vanishing footprints. I found my friend standing by a mound of snow. He'd dug some away to reveal a cairn of rocks and pebbles. We'd made it to Base Camp.
We somehow pitched our tent and made a soup (at that altitude the water took a long time to boil). In the middle of the night an ermine snuck up to snaffle our vegetable peelings. The sight of a small, furry animal, another living creature in that vast icy waste, was indescribably moving.

The next day, on our descent (we weren't seriously thinking of climbing Annapurna) we were crossing an ice-sheet when we heard a sound like thunder. We looked up to see a white wave of snow breaking down the mountain-side. Doing our best not to panic we slipped and slid across the ice. We just made it to the woods on the other side, looking back in time to see the avalanche break over the ice-sheet in plumes of snow, its irresistible force snapping the trees on the edge of the forest like sticks.

When I was young, I had the romantic notion that I'd die young – like Keats and Shelley, Jimi Hendrix and Jim Morrison – a sudden, violent, most likely drug-induced death. In old age, we come face to face with the gradual processes of death, physical decay and the waning of our powers. Unless we believe in a Vengeful Judge, we have no cause to fear the Afterlife – or our own non-existence – though it's natural to wish for a few more years in this beautiful, painful world. The challenge is in the dying itself, the act of leaving.

I pray for a good death, where I'm at peace

with the world and my loved ones and ready to let go and embark on the journey into the Great Unknown. I'm doing what I can to prepare myself, though a recent near-death experience reminded me that the circumstances of our passing are not necessarily under our control. It's hard to be stoic and unattached when you're literally suffocating.

In August 2019, in County Sligo, Ireland, I caught a severe lung-infection, which wasn't helped by being in the middle of a bog. Whenever I lay down my lungs filled with what felt like cotton-wool; I'd be gasping and coughing in a vain attempt to clear the blockage. I had to sleep sitting up, waking with a start every time my head lolled. I had no medication and it never occurred to me to call a doctor. The only things that helped were hot ginger brews – and opium, which I harvested and prepared myself from from white poppies growing wild.

The opium unlocked strange lucid dreams, which could be seen as visitations from spirit guides. I was in a waiting-room full of old people. It occurred to me that they were all 'Leavers'. At first I took that to mean they were Brexiters; then it dawned that they were waiting to leave this world and that I was there with them. But, again, my guardian angel intervened – in the form of those fairies who whisked me off to their orgy to renew my lust for life.

Since when, every day, every moment is a gift.

My first-hand experiences in The Otherworlds have convinced me that, at the very least, there exists an Astral dimension in which our thoughts and deeds take on lives of their own. I can't prove its existence, and even if I could it wouldn't provide evidence that a soul or consciousness can survive the death of the physical body. There are powerful arguments against such a proposition: our consciousness, including its ability to conceive of The Afterlife, is shaped by sense impressions, which are faculties of living organisms.

Truth is, none of us know. We can choose to believe or have faith, put our trust in atheistic materialism, or maintain a principled agnosticism. We can practice Goose and Crow Magic without investing in a belief system. We act *as if* it is so. And so it is.

In the absence of certainly, since the so-called Enlightenment and 'the Death of God', the Dream of Immortality has increasingly focused on this world. The very rich pursue Life Extension through medical and bionic advances, some looking to buy time for when the technology will allow them to make digital copies of themselves.

People like to think they'll live on through their children and descendents or, for those of us who don't have children, by passing on ideas to future generations. Even that arch-materialist Richard Dawkins recognised that biological genes had a cultural equivalent, coining the word 'memes' to describe 'a unit of cultural transmission'. I hope that something of this book will live on in you, as William Blake, John Michell and a cast of many thousands live on in me.

But what of the Ultimate Death – of our species, human culture, consciousness itself? We're all complicit in an ecological crisis which threatens our own survival and is taking many other life-forms down with us. Our work is to adapt, simplify, rebalance our lives with Life itself. To open our minds to Big Mind (No Mind) – and be part of it all.

I came here to live in the Isles of the Blessed, in the Summer-lands, in the knowledge that I may well die here. Before I do, I intend to live as fully and creatively as I can. As I hope this book testifies, my first year in Glastonbury has granted me some valuable insights and affirmations in this World and The Others.

For now, at least, Katy and I have found a place in the scheme of things. I don't want to flaunt our good fortune, especially at a time when our very existence seems so tenuous and conditional. This year, we lost loved ones: Katy's Mum, and several life-long friends. Their deaths cast shadows even on the brightest days.

This book was written as we tentatively emerged from the shadow of the Plague Year. It seeks to evoke a new world rising from the ashes of the old.

The Bards were back in St Ben's for the Winter Solstice, where the female Bard Shee performed her *Christ came by,* evoking a celestial silence at the heart of our bull-roaring Ox-pen! I did *The Ballad of Grope Cunt Lane* and the congregation saw that it was holy. We were back again for Imbolc, turning The Wheel of the year that marks the centenary of Alice Buckton's *Glastonbury – Past and Present* pageant film. For the Queen's Platinum Jubilee on Sunday 6th February 2022, The Mayor arranged a showing of the restored film, its first public screening in Glastonbury since its release a hundred years ago. And Katy and I finally got to light up the much-delayed Glastonbury Occult Conference with a talk and a workshop on Goose and Crow Magic.

New Life Pledge: to make more time and space to support Katy on her own journeys, and not always be looking to recruit her for my latest adventure. To listen and learn from her: to pay attention to the little details and to the lost Art of Mending of which she is Mistress.

This Glastonbury Year has taught me the value of grounding our Grail Quests in everyday life. It's only human to yearn to resolve all the contradictions of this world in some ultimate consummation towards which we journey. But that Apocalyptic moment is not hiding in some uncertain future. It's happening all around us.

In our quest for personal gnosis, may we never lose sight of the small beauties: Blake's 'Minute Particulars', the singing of birds and the moon in the blackthorn tree; friendship and community; small acts of care and kindness; the Divine love and magic revealed in this world, moment by eternal moment.

This is not even the end of this book. Once you've turned the page and read the spell that looses and binds, you're invited to go back and begin again. Speak the spells aloud, with intent, for healing and reconciliation in yourself and The Other.

Here in The Goose and Her shining emptiness, we invoke God and Goddess, Jesus, Mary, Michael, Mary Magdalene, Isis, Kwan Yin, Bridie, Benignus, Joseph of Arimathea and the saints of The Abbey, Arthur and Guinevere, Merlin, Taliesin, the fairy tribes of Gwyn-ap-Nudd and all the Divine Beings of the Celestial Court, to be with us in the Great Work of Healing and Transformation.

Open pathways.

In Mary. In Michael.
In their twin lines entwined.
In Mary I loose.
In Michael I bind.

In Michael. In Mary.
In matter. In mind.
In Michael be firm.
In Mary be kind.